other side river

contemporary japanese women's poetry, volume 2

THE ROCK SPRING COLLECTION OF JAPANESE LITERATURE

other

FREE VERSE

side
river

edited and translated by
leza lowitz and miyuki aoyama

The editor wishes to gratefully acknowledge the generous support of the National Endowment for the Humanities, which made the creation of this book possible. May the NEH and NEA continue to support literary and artistic projects such as this despite the insidious political forces that threaten them.

Acknowledgment is also made to the editors of the following publications in which some of these translations first appeared:
Winds, Japan Environment Monitor, Noctiluca, Printed Matter, and *Shearsman.*

Published by STONE BRIDGE PRESS
P.O. Box 8208 • Berkeley, California 94707
TEL 510-524-8732 • FAX 510-524-8711

Cover art by Karen Marquardt. Book design by Peter Goodman.

English text copyright © 1995 Leza Lowitz. Original poetry published in Japan.

Library of Congress Cataloging-in-Publication Data

Other side river: free verse / edited and translated by Leza Lowitz and Miyuki Aoyama.
    p.   cm.—(Contemporary Japanese women's poetry: v. 2)
    "The Rock Spring collection of Japanese literature."
    Includes bibliographical referencces.
    ISBN 1-880656-16-7 (pb)
    1. Japanese poetry—Women authors—Translations into English. 2. Japanese poetry— 20th century—Translations into English. I. Lowitz, Leza.   II. Aoyama, Miyuki. III. Series.
PL782.E3085   1995
895.6'150809287—dc20

95-14440
CIP

to our mothers and teachers

contents

Note to readers about Japanese names: Names of writers and other Japanese people referred to in this book appear in Western order—family name last—except for premodern literary and historical figures, who appear family name first and are customarily known by their given or "art" names. Macrons ("long signs") are used to aid pronunciation of Japanese names except for those names of writers whose published work in English regularly appears without them. In a few cases nonstandard romanizations have been used at the request of individual writers.

introduction

This collection of contemporary free verse poetry by Japanese women—emerging and famous poets ranging in age from 39 to 89—reflects a wide range of approaches to language and subject matter.

In Japan, the "freedom" of free verse these poems reflect comes not merely from the "openness" of the form. Although the very history of Japanese free verse (*shi*) dates back barely more than a century, the term *shi* itself was originally used for poems written in classical Chinese during the eighth century A.D., thus being associated with foreignness from the outset. And since the form is historically a Western "import," inspired by French modernism, it necessarily lacks the tradition-bound rules associated with *tanka* and *haiku*, Japan's traditional short verse forms that were the focus of *A Long Rainy Season*, Volume I of our anthology of contemporary Japanese women's poetry.

Flexible and new, then, relatively speaking, Japanese free verse continues to evolve and to change—to a far greater degree than tanka or haiku. As the title of this collection suggests, like a river from the "other side" to "this side" the poems here map some of those changes and chart the course of women's poetry from the years following World War II to the present day.

Although free verse poetry is considered "young" in a country of ancient poetic traditions, Japanese *women's* free verse is even younger still. Women free verse poets did not really emerge until the middle of the twentieth century. (Many of those pioneers are alive today and are included in this anthology.) The early history of Japanese free verse (no matter what gender its poets) provides a necessary perspective for assessing their work, although as Kenneth Rexroth wrote in his anthology *Women Poets of Japan,* "It should be understood that modern women free verse poets have no direct connection with mainstream changes in pre-war and post-war poetry" as they "seem to belong more to the universal stream from the medieval period than to any movement of recent decades."

With that caveat, a brief history of Japanese free verse and the social background of its evolution follows. Every era and every poetry group had its brilliant and noteworthy poets, and it is unfortunately impossible to name them all here.

THE EMERGENCE OF
FREE VERSE POETRY IN JAPAN

Historically, major movements in Japanese free verse (and modern art and architecture as well) have generally followed the introduction of Western works, gaining inspiration from those foreign works and "translating" them into Japanese forms that later evolved into native expressions. In the case of poetry, it was a series of excellent translations of Western free verse poetry that inspired Japanese poets to create new styles and to experiment in their own language. These translations also catalyzed shifts in lifestyles and values, as they continue to do to this day. Ironically, it has been Japanese formal verse (largely haiku, with its Zen sensibilities) that has inspired Western writers of modern and contemporary poetry. Some Japanese poets mixed traditional Japanese forms with modernist expressions, but free verse in Japan usually denotes poetry written in the European tradition.

The birth of Japanese *shintaishi* ("new style poetry") is associated with the 1882 publication of *Shintaishi-shō* (Anthology of New Style Poems), which contained translations of fourteen poems by Western writers as diverse as Longfellow, Tennyson, and Shakespeare (the "To Be or Not to Be" speech from *Hamlet* was included, among other excerpts) and five poems by Japanese poets written in the new style—meaning poetry in Japanese that was not tanka or haiku or even *haibun* (prose pieces that accompanied haiku in the works of Bashō and others).

The publication of the *Shintaishi-shō* anthology reflected the Japanese government's emphasis on cultural reform and nationalism—a country that had isolated itself for 250 years now needed to westernize and modernize itself to "catch up" and stay strong. This period in Japanese history, called the Meiji period (1868–1912), was marked by immense social change and sweeping reforms that brought Western medicine, jurisprudence, philosophy, and literature into Japanese daily life. It is interesting to note that the editors of *Shintaishi-shō* were not poets but professors at the University of Tokyo, and social reformers as well. One later founded modern sociology in Japan, another was a botanist who introduced Darwinism to the country, and the third became the first Japanese professor of Western philosophy. The publication and dissemination of the *Shintaishi-shō* anthology was seen as a means of accomplishing social and cultural change through language reform. The "new style" poems it contained used accessible, common words for the first time in poetry written in Japanese.

More Shakespeare and Byron as well as Goethe, Heine, and

many German poets were translated into Japanese over the next forty years. European literary movements also gained popularity in Japan, but rather than evolving slowly and naturally, they were adopted in relatively rapid succession. For example, 1894 saw the birth of Japanese romanticism with the advent of the literary magazine *Bungakukai* (Literary World). By 1897, naturalism had taken root, and by the beginning of the next century, symbolism.

Spurred by these changes was a strong movement toward the revitalization of traditional forms. Under the direction of tanka poet Tekkan Yosano (1873-1935), the magazine *Myōjō* (Bright Star) and its affiliated group of writers ushered in a new, boldly individualistic age. *Myōjō* flourished from 1900 to 1909, publishing the unabashed and sensual poetry of Akiko Yosano (who was married to Tekkan). Her turn-of-the-century tanka renewed the hope that traditional forms could reflect modern life in fresh new ways. In 1909 the Jiyūshisha (Free Verse Society) advocated abandoning traditional forms in favor of poetry that used colloquial language and realism. Soon thereafter, more and more poets gave up traditional forms and began writing *kindaishi*, or "modern poetry."

In addition to suggesting new ways of expression, Western literature also introduced Japanese writers to new ways of living and pointed up the shortcomings of Japan's rigid social structure. The Pan Society, founded in 1908, was a group of artists and writers who held "decadent" literary salons. Those who viewed poetry as an agent of social change created anthologies like *Shakaishugi Shishū* (Collection of Socialist Poetry), which was ultimately banned just after its publication in 1903.

The decisive movement to *gendaishi*, or "contemporary poetry," occurred in the Taishō period (1912–26), when poets and critics—captivated by translations of Western poetry, this time Verlaine and Baudelaire—formed a vital *avant-garde* movement. The poetry of the influential Shirakaba (White Birch) society signified a move toward humanism, inspired by the work of the American poet Walt Whitman, whose *Leaves of Grass* was translated into Japanese by one of the group's members. The magazine *Kanjō* (Feelings) was created in 1916; the new-style colloquial lyricism that appeared in its pages established the significance of this approach in poetry.

Living in a group-oriented society, most Japanese poets belonged to "poetry groups" that published their own magazines and largely defined the poet's "place" in the literary world—at least historically. Japanese free verse poets of the early Taishō period became more or less united with the formation of a large group called the Shiwakai (Poetry Discussion Association) in 1917. However, a split arose when Socialist poets emerged to form the Minshū-shi (Popular Poetry) group, active from 1917–25. The poems in the group's magazine, *Minshū* (The People), took colloquialism in language to its equivalent in content, using scenes from the everyday lives of common people as subject matter. Disagreements over the strong political nature of the Minshū-shi group's work soon surfaced, leading to the breakdown of the Shiwakai in 1921.

TOWARD A NEW
LITERATURE FOR WOMEN

By the early Taishō period, women had begun their fight for educational, legal, and social rights (this is discussed in Volume I). Women writers openly embraced these new freedoms in poems and essays, particularly those published in Japan's first feminist literary magazine, the short-lived *Seitō* (Blue Stocking), established in

1911 by Raichō Hiratsuka (1886–1971). Adding their support were popular magazines for women such as *Fujin Kōron* (Women's Forum, 1918) and *Nyonin Geijutsu* (Women's Arts, 1928). A political group, the Shinfujin Kyōkai (New Women's Association) was established in 1919 by Fusae Ichikawa and Mumeo Oku.

Early in the Shōwa era (1926–89) there were reportedly as many as 180 poetry magazines being published. New poetry groups and magazines continued to emerge, now combining social criticism and anarchism with strong experimental and dadaist tendencies that showed the influence of European modernism and the *avant-garde*. From 1928 to 1931 *Shi to Shiron* (Poetry and Poetics) was one magazine in which poetic theory played an important role, though the group disbanded due to theoretical disagreements among its members. Less theory oriented and far more adventurous was Katsue Kitazono (1902–78), one of the most influential and creative of the dadaist poets, who began his *avant-garde* magazine *VOU* in 1935 and revived it after the war in 1945.

As the seeds of the Pacific War were being sown, the nationalistic Japanese government over time forced the more critical writers into silence (the Proletarian Literature movement was disbanded in 1934, its members made to recant) while others voiced expressions of patriotism. Women were encouraged to reject modernist values and return to the Meiji-period virtues of modesty and selflessness in which service to parents, husband, and children was the paramount concern.

Between the postwar years and the beginning of the Korean War, poetry groups began to appear again, some of them resurrected from their prewar beginnings. Among those which had the greatest impact on postwar contemporary free verse poetry were VOU (named for Kitazono's magazine) and Arechi (Waste Land; the group was inspired by T. S. Eliot's 1922 poem as well as by existentialism). Another important group, not as experimental as VOU or Arechi, was Kai (Oar), started in 1953 by the intellectual poets Shuntarō Tanikawa, Makoto Ōoka, Hiroshi Kawasaki, Hiroshi Yoshino, and Noriko Ibaragi, all in their twenties.

The war had had a devastating impact on the populace, both physically and psychologically. Women were expected to help rebuild the country and to redevote themselves to providing stable family environments for children, hard-working husbands, and aging in-laws. It was young poets like Noriko Ibaragi, writing about their personal losses and the pain of war and its aftermath, who gave birth to women's free verse poetry in Japan.

WOMEN'S FREE VERSE POETRY TODAY

Many of Japan's contemporary women poets are talented musicians, composers, painters, potters, dancers, and weavers—arts they pursue in addition to writing poetry, holding down academic careers, and taking care of their families. Most of the major women poets are fully engaged in the intellectual life. While they are writing books of essays and criticism, they publish and edit magazines, teach language and literature at universities and community colleges, lecture regularly, serve as the heads of major poetry organizations in Japan and as members of major prize committees and literary societies, and organize cultural events and readings. They often translate their own works into foreign languages in addition to translating the works of writers such as Saint-John Perse, Marguerite Yourcenar, Gertrude Stein, Erica Jong, H.D., and others from French, English, Korean, and other languages into Japanese. They are credited with bringing the Beat movement, feminist poetics, and African-American studies to Japan. The reality is far different from the tired stereotype of the unliberated, behind-the-scenes Japanese woman.

The first woman to emerge in the world of free verse poetry was Kiyoko Nagase, whose emotionally unrestrained poems that captured a woman's perspective were very much a rarity in the 1930s. She was followed in the early 1950s by Noriko Ibaragi, a young intellectual and the first woman to become a "major" free verse poet. Ibaragi's poem "When I Was at My Most Beautiful" became the anthem of a generation of women who had lost the best years of their lives to the war. In Ibaragi's poetry, as in many of the Kai poets, social criticism came through lyrical, rhetorical evocations of personal suffering and not through polemics. The "Social School" of postwar poets soon counted among its members the women poets Rin Ishigaki, whose sense of justice and compassion came from the difficult forty-one years she endured working full-time at a bank to support her mother and family while writing, and Rumiko Kōra, among others. Kōra's long career as a leading poet, scholar, antiwar activist, and critic typifies the commitment of Japanese women free verse poets to social activism, politics, and change through their life's work. Many of these postwar women poets have received the most important literary prizes in Japan, and they continue to be active to this day, influencing generations of poets of both sexes through their poetry and theoretical writing and through their lifestyles.

EXPERIMENTATION
AND COMMUNITY

By the 1960s women's free verse poetry had become a distinct cultural force, and at its forefront was Kazuko Shiraishi. A student of Katsue Kitazono and a member of his VOU group that continued to inspire many young poets well after the war was over, Shiraishi revolutionized Japanese women's free verse in a number of ways. One was by taking the printed word into the realm of performance in readings with jazz musicians, Beat poets such as Kenneth Rexroth, Allen Ginsberg, Gary Snyder, and others worldwide; another was through her uninhibited eroticism and embrace of the "Other" in her poetry and counterculture lifestyle. Stylistically, she was the first to create the long poem, mixing myth and eroticism in a hypnotizing blend of stream-of-consciousness framed by a pulsating life force. Having taught and performed at poetry festivals and symposiums, universities, and concerts worldwide, Shiraishi exhibits a truly global yet intensely personal perspective, making her the best known of Japan's women poets abroad.

In later generations, the influence of the Beat Generation and the work of Kazuko Shiraishi and her predecessors can be seen in many poets like Yufuko Shima, a poet from Okinawa who mixes mystical themes with jazz rhythms; Hiroko Yoshida, whose free-spirited poetry reflects an all-embracing sensuality; and Harumi Makino Smith, for whom American jazz is a direct source of inspiration.

In the late 1960s, women poets began to form a strong literary community, often as a result of being marginalized. In 1968 the leading Japanese publisher of poetry, Shichōsha, began publishing a series of individual contemporary poets (over 125 volumes have appeared to date, 15 of them by women poets). Dozens of smaller literary magazines were established around the same time, including Sachiko Yoshihara and Kazue Shinkawa's influential Tokyo-based feminist magazine *La Mer* (known for its regular poetry readings). The magazine flourished until 1993, when the illness of one of the editors forced it to suspend operation. Shinkawa and Yoshihara are both highly respected poets and essayists (Shinkawa was president of the Japan Modern Poets' Society) who have written beautifully and openly about the war, love, women's bodies, motherhood, sexuality, guilt, betrayal, and eroticism. Their viewpoint is mature and calm, yet powerful and intense. It is no surprise that the Chinese character used for their magazine's name is a complicated wordplay based on the translation of *La Mer* ("the sea" in French). The character for *umi* ("sea" in Japanese) contains the character for "mother," thus deepening the association between the French homophones *mer* and *mère* ("mother"). The primeval sensuality and power of the sea, coupled with the warmth and nurturing of motherhood, characterizes the work of these two influential poets.

Many free verse poets have been influenced by the classical imagery of the *Manyōshū* (Anthology of Ten Thousand Leaves, ca. A.D. 780), but the focus on language is considered the central feature of contemporary Japanese free verse. Chimako Tada, a respected intellectual poet and translator, takes a philosophical approach in much of her poetry, which pursues a phenomenological inquiry into being and existence through language. Tada's work is some of the most creative and challenging poetry and prose-poetry being written today.

A strong sense of compassion and connection to the earth can be felt in the work of well-known poets Junko Takahashi, whose slightly surreal environments are suffused with a sense of spiritual depth, and Ryōko Shindō, whose poems radiate peaceful acceptance even as they project an uncertain future. Mieko Watanabe's poems share this connection to the earth, and it is often through a vividly colored landscape that her poetry's erotic or political intensity emerges. The poet and scholar Kiyoko Horiba's mythical evocation of an Inuit goddess celebrates the archetypical female in her powerful, primal glory. Saho Asada, one of the few lesbian poets writing about her sexuality in Japan today, celebrates her love for women and expresses the hope that lesbian poets can emerge from the closet.

Inspired by symbolism, surrealism, the spare power of the imagist poets, and Gertrude Stein's cubism (among other styles and schools), poets such as Chimako Tada and Michiko Yamamoto have created fantastical prose poems, or *sanbunshi*, whose styles echo the prose diaries of the Heian court poet Sei Shōnagon. The inheritor of this style in the 1980s and 1990s is the young poet Toshiko Hirata, whose poems, often in prose-poem form, explore a peculiar obsession with identity and belonging, materialism and matter, and exude a quirky warmth that borders on the lighthearted. She also artfully employs regional dialect. Experimentation with language, both visually and in terms of musicality, is evident in the soft-focus, fantastical, dreamlike imagery of later poets such as Teruko Kunimine, Masayo Koike, Michiyo Nakamoto, and others included in this anthology. Miyuki Aoyama has taken the theme of motherhood and employed it structurally in nine-line poems inspired by Sylvia Plath and written during pregnancy, while her poems' content reflects an increasingly apocalyptic landscape.

LANGUAGE, FRAGMENTATION, AND INTELLECTUALISM

The early 1970s brought antiwar protests, debates over the Japan-U.S. Security Treaty, and the student movement to college campuses. The advent of the "me-decade" and the strong personalities of many of Japan's women poets now made poetry groups less significant than they were in the prewar and immediate postwar periods. It was around this time that Taeko Tomioka, whose strong feminist stance and experimentation with a female-centered language had created a sensation in the previous decade, stopped writing poetry. Tomioka's long poems often contain highly ambiguous narrative structures and complex dialogues in which a speaker or narrator emerges. Yet the speaker of the poetic dramatic monologues can not necessarily be identified as the author herself. Poems such as these, in which the language encompasses a variety of perspectives, can be seen as a kind of literary *ukiyo-e*, a verbal analogue to Japan's woodblock prints, so highly prized for their shifting scenes and vantage points. Yohko Isaka, an important feminist poet, took Tomioka's complex narrative structure and used it in her poems detailing the sexual exploits of high school girls in the 1970s and in her later verse as well.

Sex is a common subject among Japanese women free verse poets today, but unlike the poets of the fifties exploring passion and eroticism, or the sixties celebrating sexual freedom, the women free verse poets of the seventies and eighties have reappropriated women's bodies and turned an exploratory eye on them. Often the approach is clinical. Isaka's poems, for example, often concern rather matter-of-fact descriptions of sexuality and lust; their frankness is startling. Like the American L=A=N=G=U=

A=G=E Poets, the women poets of recent years have created within each poem a self-defined reality, one that need not reflect or speak to an "outside" reality. They have described the ordinary world of work, home, school, procreation by means of a woman-centered language. Since the 1960s, language has taken on increasing importance in Japanese free verse poetry. Structurally, the line has broken down into blocks of text, into poems that could be prose or vice-versa, within which language slammed into itself and the syntax was often unclear, verging on incomprehensibility.

This fragmentation was evident in Japanese society as well. For example, in a country where youth do not often rebel, the 1980s were a period of unprecedented violence within Japanese high schools. But with the Japanese economy finally stable, many Japanese women were able to turn to the community, supporting school functions and engaging in social activities with their children. Home is still where many Japanese women spend most of their time, and it is a place of special concern to experimental feminist poet Hiromi Itō, who, influenced by feminist theorists like Julia Kristeva, Melanie Klein, and others, explores domesticity and the female body through fragmentation in language. Itō often writes poems in which the speaker/poet engages in a poetic dialogue or conversation with a *doppelgänger*—a different person bearing the same name, or a split self, or "another half."

The dichotomies of public and private are also split open in Itō's work, and the body itself, particularly the female body, is subject to dissection. Itō puts the female body—defecating, menstruating, reproducing, ovulating, lactating, masturbating—under the microscope and records its activities with a kind of clinical detachment that is a mixture of disgust and fascination. To a degree found in no other young poet in Japan today, Itō's graphic descriptions of bleeding, death, mutation, and bodily functions reflect a fascination with the brutal and the grotesque as somehow beautiful, a fascination that might be characterized as reflecting distinctly Japanese concerns. In Itō's poems, it is the female body that is exposed and magnified, perhaps for the same reason that the *ukiyoe* prints of the latter half of the eighteenth century show massively enlarged genitalia: the Japanese artist has a penchant for isolating an element of the subject so it can be explored in minute detail. This focus on the body has an important social aspect as well. Think of the *samurai* penchant for disemboweling and decapitation. It was, after all, the horrors of atomic weapons and incendiary bombing during the war that made the absolute frailty and impermanence of the human body a focus of national concern in Japan. Some contemporary poets describe the physical horrors of World War II from a personal and explicit perspective dealing with loss and memory. Examples in this anthology include Tsuneko Yoshikawa's poem about a poet experiencing the horror of the atomic bombing of Hiroshima, and Ritsuko Kawabata's quiet laments for lost family members.

Another feature of poetry in the 1980s is the nihilism of the individual-in-the-late-twentieth-century-detachment-from-everything stance—including detachment from one's own body and its functions, even as they are dissected and isolated. In Itō's poems, pleasure is not even an issue: incantatory, repetitive, chantlike, the poems often reflect the literal breakdown of the human being in an increasingly mechanized and technological world. The poems of Toshiko Hirata, which can also be "unintelligible" or syntactically unclear, reflect a particularly 1980s obsession with things, a universe of objects that presumably define oneself but fail to do much more than stage a relentless assault on the senses.

The death of Emperor Hirohito in 1989 and the beginning of the Heisei era in Japan opened the way for a great deal of previously suppressed criticisms and reevaluations of the past. Japanese women today have a different sense of their "Japaneseness" and greater expectations for what life has to offer. Instead of devoting themselves solely to husbands and children, they are more interested in foreign travel, in consumerism, and in finding a profession. Like Japanese male poets and intellectuals in the Meiji period, many Japanese women poets today travel or live abroad and write eloquently about their experiences. An interesting offshoot of this phenomenon is that many Japanese women free verse poets are actually choosing to write in English, as they feel it gives them more freedom of expression and removes cultural baggage. Among others, Yuri Kageyama, Fumiko Tachibana, and Kiyoko Ogawa have all lived and traveled outside Japan and write a great deal of their poetry in English (including the poems that appear in this book). Keiko Matsui Gibson writes with irony and warm humor about the cross-cultural issues a Japanese woman faces living in America. Many others, like Kazuko Shiraishi, participate often in international poetry festivals and have had a powerful impact abroad.

THE "OUTSIDERS" WITHIN

The government of Japan typically presents the country as composed of "one race," but this is a myth perpetuated largely by the imperial system to foster uniformity. In fact there are many different peoples. The consequences of being different in Japan are severe, however. Poets from three groups that face discrimination in Japan appear in this anthology to give voice to their world through their poetry. "Language" is also a central aspect of their poems, but here, language is both a tool and a weapon. Chuwol Chong is a poet who writes poignantly and unapologetically about her experience as a second-generation *zainichi*, or Korean "resident of Japan," and her struggle to find an identity. The first generation of Koreans were forcibly brought to Japan as laborers during the period of Japanese colonialization that began in 1910 and lasted until the end of World War II. After 1939, Koreans sent to Japan to work were forced to take Japanese names and to give up their Korean names; by losing their Korean names they essentially were made to hide or deny their culture. After the war they were legally free to return home. Most, however, had by then established a life in Japan, and leaving would have been difficult if not impossible. Koreans who remained in Japan were required to use their Japanese names until 1947, when they were allowed to take up their real (Korean) names again.

Since prejudice and discrimination against *zainichi* remains widespread and deep-rooted, many of Japan's nearly 700,000 Koreans have chosen to conceal their origins and use Japanese names instead. If they wish to keep their Korean names, they must register as "foreigners," even if they were born in Japan. Until recently, Koreans in Japan had to have their fingerprints on their Alien Registration Cards. Chuwol Chong's poem "Two Names" addresses the poet's struggle with her history and the dual identities *zainichi* are forced to live with. Her other poems describe the hard realities of the present and her dreams of a better future for the generations to come. Also included here is a poem by Kyong Mi Park, a third-generation Japanese of Korean ancestry, who writes about her pride and shame at seeing a woman wearing a traditional Korean dress in downtown Tokyo.

The poet Mieko Chikapp, a weaver and human rights activist, is an Ainu. The Ainu are the indigenous people of Japan; currently they number about 25,000. Originally a hunting and fishing culture settled throughout northern Japan, the Ainu now live mostly in the farther north: in Hokkaido, Sakhalin, and the Kuril Islands. Scientists are unsure as to their exact origins, but the Ainu are thought to be related to Europeans, Asians, or even the Aboriginese of Australia. During the Edo period, the Ainu were massacred by the Matsumae clan acting on behalf of the ruling Tokugawa shogunate. In 1867 the shogunate fell and was replaced by the Meiji government, which colonized the Ainu and took away their land. The Ainu were forced to relocate and abandon their traditions to become farmers, but the lands they were given were mostly unfit for cultivation and were taken away from them if they could not turn them into farmland within a fifteen-year period. The government first began a program of economic aid for the Ainu in the 1970s. Mieko Chikapp is at the forefront of the fight for Ainu human rights, and her poems reflect this struggle and hope using Ainu language and myth.

Misao Fujimoto and Iro Kitadai are from the caste of "untouchables" called *burakumin.* Although they are not "professional" poets, their strong poems call out for inclusion here. Ethnically and racially *burakumin* are Japanese, but they have been the object of severe social discrimination and residential segregation owing to their occupations, which in the past involved "unclean" tasks such as tanning, butchering, and caring for the dead. Their status as outcastes was formalized in the late sixteenth century by the Tokugawa shogunate. Today, except for the exalted rank of the emperor and the imperial family, all castes have been legally abolished in Japan. But Japan is still a class-conscious society, and this is reflected in rituals of speech, bowing, gift giving, and other easily observed social interactions. Likewise, many of Japan's nearly 3 million *burakumin* continue to live in designated *buraku,* or "hamlets." And discrimination against them continues, overtly in the form of illegal background checks by corporations and potential spouses, and just as insidiously in the process by which lack of opportunity in education, housing, and the workplace is passed down from generation to generation. Educational opportunity is a primary focus of groups like the Buraku Liberation League. Fujimoto's and Kitadai's poems describe their encounters with the Japanese language after a lifetime of illiteracy and the new power and hope that learning to read has given them. Theirs is certainly a stance vastly different from that of the poets reworking the Japanese language in their poems and provides an interesting perspective.

A NOTE ON SELECTION AND TRANSLATION

Modern Japan has thousands of amateur poets, and many experts in other professions write poetry as a hobby, including Nobel Prize–winning scientists and department-store scions. In addition to the thousands of magazines published and disseminated among poets and their poetry groups, readings and performances are held frequently, especially in large cities like Tokyo. Still, writing poetry is a relatively isolated endeavor, and there is a sense of alienation from poets outside of one's own "group." Recently, too, a thematic shift has occurred in women's poetry: where poems used to be about "landscape" and country, many Japanese poems now are more about the family, the individual, and the "house" of the individual—that is, the body—as a landscape or country of its own.

Yes, poetry is booming in Japan today, but as noted scholar and translator Hiroaki Sato has pointed out, there is a "division of labor" in contemporary Japanese poetry, insofar as those who write tanka write only tanka and those who write haiku tend to stick to that form. Likewise, those who write *gendaishi*, or "contemporary poetry," do not tend to write in any other genre. Several women free verse poets, for example Hiromi Itō and Toshiko Hirata, two of the leading poets of the new generation, do write prose and essays that often border on being prose poetry. The forms are alive, thriving and mutating daily.

The original objective of both volumes of this anthology of contemporary Japanese women's poetry was to introduce the most important living women poets of Japan to Western readers. In the Introduction to Volume I I mentioned the difficulty of this notion of "importance," and that many "important" poets were no longer active or writing at the top of their form. I also mentioned the humility of some younger poets as well as the snobbishness of some of the established writers affecting their willingness to be a part of this project. Some women poets in Japan seem to have lost a spirit of solidarity. Of course, this is true elsewhere in the world as well.

In an effort to represent the current state of Japanese women's poetry today, renowned and unknown poets, "professionals" and "amateurs" alike are included here. We tried to include poets from all over Japan—not just from Tokyo, and not just those living in major metropolitan areas. Despite our best efforts, there were some poets whom we would have liked to include but for reasons too numerous to list could not. It should be said, then, that as with any selection this one is not definitive. Undoubtedly there are poets who have been left out, poems that should have been included but weren't, and poets whose inclusion will be controversial. We chose poets by recommendation and personal taste, and in some cases discovered a poet in a literary publication or through an introduction.

As for selecting the poems, we asked the poets themselves to do the initial sorting. Knowing that their work would be translated into English, which of their poems, spanning their careers, did they want Western readers to discover? Many manuscripts arrived in handwritten bundles. Although we wanted only previously untranslated poems, we discovered that some poets, unbeknownst to us, and in some cases, unbeknownst to the poet herself, had given us work that had already been translated or scheduled for translation into English. In some cases, when a poem was particularly important historically, such as Noriko Ibaragi's "When I Was at My Most Beautiful," we translated it, knowing it had already been published in a different English version.

As in Volume I, the poems here were translated through collaboration and extensive rewriting. Miyuki Aoyama translated the first drafts of all the poems (except those noted as translated by Akemi Tomioka) and together we rewrote and edited the works, adopting a faithful but nonliteral approach in order to capture the spirit of the original verse as we saw it. Punctuation and stylistic decisions were made for each poem individually. Of course, all responsibility for the translations is ours. (Having come to the end of this project, I now believe that there are some contemporary Japanese poets who just cannot be translated successfully into English. This is partly due to a certain syntactical ambiguity, or even "unintelligibility," but also to the deeply cultural associations and reverberations of the Japanese language that are impossible to recreate in English.)

Historically, it has been a dialogue with Western poetry that has inspired the emergence and growth of "free verse" poetry in Japan. Until now, the dialogue has been fairly one-sided. Few contemporary Japanese poets have been translated into English—most of the women poets in this book, when they have been published in English at all, have done the translations themselves in self-published volumes, with a few notable exceptions. With the publication of this anthology, we hope to open further avenues of exchange, understanding, and appreciation.

ACKNOWLEDGMENTS

First and foremost, thanks to Akemi Tomioka for her excellent translations in this volume, for her commitment to bringing a diverse range of poets to its pages, and for her boundless energy in making it happen; to Tatemi Sakai of the Orion Literary Agency for his prize-worthy efforts on our behalf; to Mieko Watanabe for the introduction of several wonderful poets we would not have otherwise learned about; and to Peter Goodman of Stone Bridge Press for just about everything we can think of in helping to see this project through.

Special thanks for support, sustenance, guidance, and love to Junko Abe, Sachiko Aoyama, Tazuko Aoyama, Toru Arai, Christopher Blasdel, Tom Chapman, Abigail Davidson, George Evans, Maryann Fleming, Elizabeth Floyd, Kathleen Fraser, Geraldine Harcourt, Jane Hirshfield, Edgar Honteschläger, Ed and Chako Ifshin, Yurika Kimijima, the Lowitzes, Peter McMillan, the Mendelsohns, Kyoko Michishita, Misao Mizuno, Hitomi Murokami, Shogo Oketani, Sherry Reniker, Donald Richie, Richard Ruben, Motoyuki and Hitomi Shibata, Kazuko Shiraishi,

Leslie and Grayson Stanford, Mihoko Sugiura, Momoko Wata-
nabe, and Laura Weiss. Finally, thanks to Miyuki Aoyama, the best
partner I could have hoped for in the world, to the poets them-
selves, whose words continue to challenge and inspire, and to you,
dear reader, for joining us here.

Leza Lowitz
San Francisco
Spring 1995

OTHER

SIDE

RIVER

miyuki aoyama

SPRING

under the cherry blossoms, warmed by the earth's smell
a man is hanging from a rope
his eyelids convulse
the man drifts in and out of his dreams
a girl's taut breasts softly grow rounder
the snake he saw yesterday returns
and eases up the trunk of the tree
the man's grip releases
many things have been thrown at his feet
on the tip of his swaying fingers
one transparent petal remains

FEBRUARY

the field of wheat is drying out
the field mouse has shriveled up

i see the teeth in its half-opened mouth
in the dead of the night
a cat with a distorted body leaps and leaps
the cat moans in a baby's voice
a woman with a low temperature slowly strolls the field
hearing the woman's footsteps
the flesh underfoot grows sullen

PEACH

a ripe peach falls
the peach sinks in the heavy summer air
a stifling hot wind pushes it up from under
a woman in her ninth month digs a hole
i put a slippery thing in my mouth
and feel sudden nausea
a woman gives out a scream behind the dark shoji
all at once, the children become sleepy
the blackened peach in the air
the dog with a black penis slowly goes crazy

saho asada

VIVA LESBIANS!

Ms. R—
A young lesbian, a teacher of Japanese, and a poet
Went to a poetry gathering and suddenly shouted:
    For myself and for my honor,   I say
    Viva lesbians! Viva lesbians!
She cries out these words only when she goes mad.
She speaks infant words with the sky blue eyes of an infant.

The most troubled by this is the great Ms. T,
Said to be a sharp knifelike poet of love.
She says:
    I'm a closet lesbian,
    And will live and die as such.
To her, "Viva lesbians!" must
Be a kind of double-edged sword.

Another woman, a Korean, writes:
When you spoke your mother tongue back then,

you were raped and killed for it.
When a young woman, a "comfort woman"*
escaped from the mental hospital
after the war, she cried out:
    I am Korean!
    I am really a Korean!

Let's keep our sanity and say,
    I am Korean!
    I am lesbian!
Let's bring in a new age.
    Viva lesbians!

WALK

If the gentle roundness of our arms
Around the napes of each other's necks
Quietly adorns our two naked bodies,
Beating in the dark of night,
Like garlands of benediction
On a long journey—
We can start walking
To where the earth becomes round.

At the twenty-sixth hour
Something like invisible snow

Soundlessly falls and stays,
Making the earth brighter than any dawn.
Then we can remember clearly
Everything that shines
We can cross the river easily.
It is the nocturnal river
Cutting through the headlands
That have witnessed our footprints.

mieko chikapp

A WINDBORNE POSTCARD

everything on earth
that has *form*
has spirit:
moon stars woods lakes,
flowers trees birds and all

when women who believed so embroidered
searching for the image of the spirit,
they came to make the image of living God
each stitch made into peculiar abstract patterns
becoming the image of the spirit.

a young woman sang *yaishamena* to herself
sighing for her lover with each stitch
she gave her lover that embroidered *tekunpe*
and her lover gave to her a *makiri*
as tokens of their love.*

now the lovers' sweet whispers are heard
on the bracing wind.
the women's embroidery of Mother Nature
are made while longing for their beloved ones.

I will send you a postcard
with this Ainu pattern
for the sake of these splendid women and men,
living and dying
for love.

chuwol chong

TWO NAMES

From my adherence to
I-am-ME and you-are-YOU,
I have always run away to crowds of strangers,
Where sleeves rub against each other
Mixing, fighting, gasping for breath.
In the sickening smell of humanity
Have I continuously walked.
But I feel as if all of that happened before yesterday,
That was *zainichi*:
"Resident of Japan."

When I came into this world,
My body received two names:
My Japanese name—a *nom de guerre*
And my real name, collateral for *zainichi*,
Printed on a card in a pocketbook with number bestowed
And fingerprints dedicated.

Was there a self who managed to remain,
Barely surviving through Japanese history?
Or was this the dreadful self
That was a product of Japanese history?
I was given the wisdom to
Live, live now, live on in any way possible
By fathers and mothers who lived through hell,
By fathers and mothers who died in it.
I have cheated on their wisdom.
Have I once gazed into the slight ripple
In my calm exterior
Resulting from the fact
That my fake name is the only weapon
Testifying to my existence?
Have I once gazed into ME,
Trembling with fear to realize YOU?

I placed a bet
That your naive smiling face,
Where innocence and ignorance mingle,
Would either quickly freeze
Or become extinct.
That was YOU.
I had to tell YOU
My real name.
I used it as a trump card.
That was ME until only yesterday.
Fathers and mothers who came across the sea,

Fathers and mothers who did not return to the sea,
You are the last people who, with the *nom de guerre* on your
    head,
Still stand by your distinctive heterodoxy.
I have no heterodoxy to stand by.
It's not honorable heterodoxy just to exist
In the presence of their particular manners,
Their particular Japanese accents,
Their particular dialects.
The names engraved on the tombs of the last people
Emit light even in a crowd of people,
Are the truth engraved in the foreign land
Where they died, the absolute truth,
Carrying weight even after death
Sending an apalling cry up
From the depths of the earth!
I must catch in my ears
And hear in my guts the silent cry
Of these weak but brave people.
I must engrave into myself
That the last people are my fathers and mothers
And I am their child, that I am ME.
I am Chong. I am Song. I am Kim. I am Pyon.
I am Lee. I am Cho. I am Pak. I am Pu.
I am Hwang. I am Ko. I am Im. I am Sin.
I am Paek. I am
From the innocent, ignorant, "gentle" Japanese

You must be set free.
From the fear of weathering
and a guilty conscience,
I must be set free.
Carrying my hell-name
In my hands, on my shoulders,
Bringing it 'round and holding it in my arms.
I still hope for the day
When we can accept each other and live openly
When we can openly accept YOU and ME.
Come, spring.
Come soon.

A WILL

Standing firmly on the withered grass of the winter field,
I feel the warmth of the earth under my feet,
The hidden life of dandelion, chickweed, and mugwort.
As the seasons come around my life spins new lives.
How pathetically green they are . . .
I want to eat up all their laughter, tears, and anger.
Gust of wind, convey to my children
Who will someday stand deep in the visionary wilderness,
That their mother was a protective and enduring grass
Against frost.

MY VISIONARY COUNTRY
(As imagined from a picture)

No scene or scenery surprises me;
I can imagine it, or I think I can.
My visionary country
Is of the piercingly high sky,
The piercingly deep water,
And the tang of red peppers.
The scene of children playing naked in the summer
Secretly changes to that of my childhood, overlapping.
But that doesn't mean I had the same childhood as they did.
But always, my visionary country lives within me
As real as it can be.
I rejoice in its joy,
And suffer in its pain.

THE SAD HISTORY
OF THE SOLE-PASTING WOMAN

From when was it, I wonder,
That my days were drowned in bliss and mirth?

I didn't seek a vocation,
Nor was I given a chance to find one;
I was to paste on the soles of sandals.
Yet my palms were not tough enough

To grip the tools that I would be embarrassed by,
I was astounded to find such tough labor
Beyond my ability,
I was frightened
By this vocational disease
That froze my blood.
I licked sandal soles all day long.
The smoke sucked into the small ventilator
Choked me.
I was drowned in glue
And paint thinner.
But my family didn't complain
About my smell, for
I was the breadwinner.
I worked on a commission
Which spurred me on.
I hid pincers within my wedding dress,
Gripped my roller even after marriage.
I continued to work for my children.
Ah, I who came after myself. I, who
Decline has caught up to,
Give my aching body healing.
Me and my many rotten aprons.
Me and the factory eaves
Who compete with each other in decaying.
I, who have lived my life with this glue
I, dizzy with the smell,
I, at my death at last,
Can go to true Paradise.

POET'S NOTE: There must be few people on this earth who have a vocation they were born to perform. Crawling shamefully on the ground, I've lived a life where I had to work like this to earn my daily bread. My work as such is glued to my body and mind. There is a reason why I can dare to say: "I didn't seek a vocation/Nor was I given a chance to find one." The Japanese are not the only people to reject differences. I too, am extremely ashamed of myself and shudder to think that I might have been the murderer of handicapped people or those with Hansen's Disease. The rejection of differences that is common throughout the Japanese Islands has its strongest origins in World War II. Thus one can clearly see, historically, why the *zainichi* system exists. Yet the myth of the pure-blooded Japanese attempts to wipe out differences. The fact that World War II was a war of aggression has been denied over and over again by many Japanese.

I've lived all my life as a *zainichi*. I accept as a matter of course the fact that in Japanese society *zainichi* aren't able to find jobs to support even the barest subsistence.

You—read aloud my short poems telling of the typical life of a *zainichi* woman and feel their resignation.

You.

SLEEP, MY GOOD CHILD
(Lullaby No. 1)

Sleep, my good child.
Sleep, my good child.

This is not a lullaby
By Brahms, Schubert, or Mozart.
Nor is it a lullaby sung
Of Itsuki or Shimabara.
It's a lullaby rocking me, rocking me,
In a bamboo basket
On a rainy afternoon
In the corner of a rain-drenched dirt floor,
Kicked by the toes of one foot
Lowered against the correct manner of sitting,
Hands not resting
From the work of thrashing straw.
I hang on to the bamboo basket
Tied to a rough-hewn rope,
Hanging from the beam
Reaching just above the straw mat.
Sleep, my good child.
Sleep, my good child.
This is a lullaby,
Tolling my mother's existence
Only for my nap.

Waiting for him in the room
Of a crumbling apartment house
Next to the roadway.
I hold my milkless breasts in my arms,
And dream of biting into him.
I fall asleep and wake up
In that position.
Trucks vibrate,
Becoming a lullaby,
Rocking me, rocking me.
Spring and fall,
Summer and winter,
The frozen air covers
The Japanese faces that his mother in kimono
Reminds me of.
I trace the air
By timidly registering my fingerprints.
Buried in the bamboo basket
Where I kick my secret monster,
Is my lullaby,
Rocking me, rocking me.
My phantom children,
Nestling close to me to fall asleep,
Are many.
My sufferings born of bitterness
Against my mother
For not having aborted me
Are many.

He doesn't clasp his hands in prayer
To the Jizō* statues in the field,
He just repeats the sacred name of Amitabha.
It might be said that he and I were born
In the same country, so that together
We could nurse the fact.
But how achingly empty that idea is.
Imagination swells my womb into a drum,
Which I joyfully keep on drumming.
It rolls like a show at a merry festival.
I must drag my lullaby along,
I can't choose it or throw it away.
Sleep, my good child.
Sleep, my good child, for
It's colder toward morning.

misao fujimoto

KANA

I've always hated *kana*.*
They've always caused me humiliation.
Whenever I was told to write my name
I flushed with shame, my hand trembled.
I have been put to shame for thirty years.
Now, our teacher teaches us *kana*.

I will learn you as quickly as I can
and use you.

keiko matsui gibson

SERENADE

In bed
between turning left and right
I dream:
origami cranes
untie themselves to sleep
cactus needles soften and wilt
moved, blue tears fall from my eyes

abruptly, my life
rests on the bottom.

KENNETH REXROTH'S EPIPHANY

You disappeared too modestly
like an autumn leaf falling invisibly.

Your powerful torso and pink face
composed a painting by Matisse
your *ramen* tasted as if Marichiko herself had boiled it.
the Womb Mandala   red and red and red
symbol of the organic universe
was your natural home.
You were a fiery Buddha, a raging *fudō-myōō* *
loving tangled Japanese hair.
I felt small beside you,
your beaming power quieted me,
you called me Keiko-san soulfully
your eloquence a sword
piercing snobbish masks
cracking the ice of authority
along the winter lakeshore.

When your moon was waning
you changed from giant to dwarf
wires taped to your stomach
choking up phlegm—
everything about you
overwhelmed me with sadness
but your eyes were more eloquent than ever
you did not let me blink.
I held your thin hands and gazed at you
I saw Carol-san kissing your lips sacredly
time and space froze

I forgot how to move my feet
I forgot how to breathe
you became a star on June 6
in Orion, your constellation.

Hope you take a long bath
in eternally consoling moonlight.

HOW DO YOU LIKE AMERICA?

Taking off from Osaka
I saw my mother standing
with a handkerchief over her eyes
and my father trying to hide
a hole in his heart-mind
then my country blurred.

For seven years I heard:
where do you come from?
China? Korea? Japan?
How long have you been in America?
Is your family still in Japan?
I bet they sure miss you!
Did you meet your husband there?
Does he speak Japanese?

You speak English very well!
Where did you learn to speak it?
How do you like America?
I pity, fear, and love it.
America is huge and sick
optimistic and terrifying
immature but lovable.

These friendly American questions
dislocated my Japanese bones.
I answered automatically
like a salivating dog
I was born in Kyoto, Japan.
It's a modern, ancient city.
I've been in America since
Jimmy Carter was president.
My parents are still in Osaka.
Because I am an only child
we miss each other a lot.
I met my husband at a bus stop
near Osaka University
where he taught.
He has been learning Japanese
ever since.
I have studied English
since I was fourteen.
Though I am working on a Ph.D.
English is still very strange.

How do I like America?
I like America very much!
It's a beautiful country!
People are kind and friendly!
Life is so comfortable here!
Heaters keep us warm!
Not many people smoke compared to Japan!

So you are from Japan?
My son married a Korean
who eats kimchi even after eating pancakes
it's unbelievably spicy!
Do you like it too?
My husband was in Japan after the war and loved it!
I used to know a Japanese girl in Hawaii
She invited me for sushi and the tea ceremony
Her name was Keeko too
Her hair was so straight and black
Such a cute little thing.
Japan is one of the places I'd like to visit sometime
It must be beautiful.
My mother does flower arranging in Traverse City
How do you like America?

How do I like America?
These cheerful Americans
much better at talking than listening
throw balls persistently without catching any

flash commercials of their lives
life goes on in many entangling circles
Americans are hectic and confusing.
When do they calm down?
The land is airy, spacious, masculine
with no canes to hold on to, to stick to:
you can draw your own road where you wish
it's a country of gushing power,
uncontrollable.

Suspended between Japan and America
stranger in both lands
alienating every being
I have stayed awake all night
hearing the drips of
Japan/America
Japan/America
Japan/America.

I have lost myself many times
eroded by changing dogmas
my friend A. became a separatist lesbian
leaving me like an old towel under the sink
my friend B. a conservative pro-family housewife
insists the only womanly virtues are pleasing her husband
and producing many children
C. can't really find a steady job because he has long hair like
    a little girl

and really believes in his poetry
D. is always frustrated about her health and family,
worries in a suffocating room without windows.
My friend E., embittered by the political impasse,
arrogantly retires to nature to be a weekend hermit.
My friend F. still plays like a kid
dreaming of making money to buy perpetual comfort.

Divorce has forced
many children to fly through the air
helpless and resentful, their hearts beating in vain.
The word "marriage" rings hollow.
The family is replaced by therapists.
People consume their energy
in jogging, aerobics, and health clubs
But where is the food that's needed
on the other side of the world?
People dread fat more
than nuclear bombs.

In Japan I was suffocated
panting for sheer freedom
but here I suffer from too much air
too chaotic to feel freedom.

My honeymoon with America has ended
something has ended.
I am ready for a separation.

America is blurring.
Just as we cannot count snowflakes
I cannot count my Karma
piling up over the Pacific.

My parents are opening their eyes.
They see me winging to them.
In Japan I will speak again
transparently, as I wish
to my mother, father, and strangers
I simply want the warmth of hands
I want tears turning into a river.

toshiko hirata

LOOKS LIKE I'LL BE A SPY

My lover has a wife
who decorates the dining room table
her cooking's pretty tasteless
and her flowers are wilting
but even so
she gets pretty passionate in bed.

They've had a baby girl
I thought I'd kidnap it
she could rub my shoulders
and I'd give her a manicure in exchange.
She could have been a substitute for my lover
but that girl looks just like his wife
and she's not what you'd call bright.

You, getting married like a fish
whose name changes as it grows

you changed it so flippantly
my sweetheart!
From a one-way perspective
or a two-way perspective
I can't see you anywhere
in these three square meters
so I'll have to call this place
a barren landscape
that your absence has stripped.

Well, it looks like I'll be a spy
wearing the brim of my hat down over my eyes
I'll record your voice with a hidden mike
and keep it in the freezer
sometimes I'll take it out and put it to my ear.
When my eyes are closed,
it'll be just like you're here.

Where we live, people sleep at night
but the light in your bedroom goes on
then is slowly shut off
I got bitten by a dog
and can't move my leg
so I watch that light like an apparition
sewed up by the silk of the night.

MY MOST EXQUISITE COLOR

Yeah, I'm only an insignificant traffic light
standing on a one-way, two lane road
with an elementary school on my right,
convenience store, liquor store, and a few houses on my left
I'm only a boring, stupid traffic light,
radiating red, blue, and yellow over and over
Like a cheap tricolored lunchbox.

It's not that I don't like the cars and drivers
who sometimes cluck their tongues at me, ready to move at
    my will.
It's just that by inhaling lots of exhaust and sweat
I've ruined my respiratory system.

You see, I'm suffering from insomnia
And am quite well suited to this job.

Birds, out on the town for thrills
conspire with me, taking pleasure in attacking
teary-eyed cowards of cars. We like to
let cars that drag children in their rear wheels
get away. Of course
I wipe up the blood.

When the smell of the sea that's not supposed to be here
Comes to me through the wind,
I stop to think, wishing

I'd been born as a lighthouse.
But showing off my pale skin
and being looked at by ships every day
is not my style.

I don't want to be loved by anyone.
When the falling rain collects,
when the road takes on the shore,
entranced by my reflection.

A pole across the street misunderstands me
Sending me a silly, stinging electric current.
Of course, I ignore him. I don't
want to love anyone.

I keep my most exquisite color a secret, don't show
it to men or cars. The day I'll reveal it
is in the still-dark morning
when I quit my job forever and get carried away.

The first and final color
is not for anyone but me.
A light like a will.
A flash like a monologue.

That's when I'll finally recover
from my happy insomnia
at last.

SNAFU

Basically, there are seven clocks in this room. Each hand points in its respective direction. Each hand points to respective numbers. One hand points to 1:10 a.m. Another points to 1:15. Another to 1:21. Another to 1:13. One to 1:02 and still another to 1:15. I'm thinking oh, this clock says the same time as the other one did, but the one that pointed to 1:15 at first now points to 1:17. One of them points to 6:45. I'm not sure if it is 6:00 a.m. or 6:00 p.m. It is a clock whose batteries wore out several years ago. The clock died at 6:45. I can't rely on the dead clock's time. I'm going to disregard the time on the dead clock's face.

There are seven clocks and if six are still alive, it is somewhere between 1:02 a.m. and 1:21 a.m. now. I wonder if 1:02 and 1:21 are the same time. What is the difference between them? The difference is not easily explained. What is obvious is that you are not here now.

In other words, you are not here. You are in the not-with of this room. Where are you? There are four calendars in this room. Three of them say it is the 6th and one of them says it is the 7th. Which doesn't mean that it is the 6th and not the 7th. After all, the date is not determined by majority rule. Furthermore, I am the one who is in charge of changing the desk pads daily. What I do is not always right. I am often wrong. There is evidence of this in that one of the pages dated the 6th is a Monday, while another is a Wednesday and the last is a Saturday. I wish it were Saturday today. Saturdays and Sundays are when I don't have to ride the subway and go up to the 13th floor of the office building. I'm scared to go into the building. I'm scared to go in the elevator because it is possessed, maybe by the devils. It is often jammed by the possessors playing tricks on us.

I wish it were Saturday today. Saturday is the day when I go to the dentist's. I don't like the dentist's but I'd rather go to the dentist's than ride that elevator.

Basically, I have been trying to determine the month for some time now. It might be November, but there is no way of proving this. There is a stove next to me, though no fire has been started. If I made a fire I could get warm.

My legs are cold. If I do not light a fire, it is of no consequence. It is not so cold that a fire is imperative. It is most likely November now, but I cannot be sure. There is an air conditioner in the adjacent room. If I turn it on, cold air will blast out of it instantly and I'll feel the cool. But I do not particularly think that wind is what I need.

Basically, the thermometer registers 17 degrees. 17 degrees is the proper temperature for November, but the temperature does not always reach 17 degrees in November. It rises to 17 degrees in April and even in May. It could be April now.

Basically, my memory tells me you are living with me here. In the morning you leave at 8:05 and you return late at night. We have been living in this way for some time. I wonder if my memory can be trusted. I wonder if this happened a long time ago, and if you have already left this place.

After leaving here, did you go to live with someone else somewhere? Or are you and I going to live together? Next year, after the new year begins and the flowers are in bloom, will we live here? Did we promise each other that we would? Or did you die a long time ago? Have we lived here for some ten years, and did you suddenly die a few years ago? Am I left alone? Why did you die? Was it from sickness? An accident?

Basically, I can't recall how old I am. I found an I.D. card in my drawer. It says I am 15 years old. Does that mean I am 15 now? Only 15? I must study for entrance exams. I must practice vaulting the horse at the gym. Does this mean you were a dream? Does this mean that I have never met you? Will I meet you after many, many years? Will I meet you when I am 23, eight years from now? It gives my birth date as June 30th, the 30th of June in the Shōwa era. I do not know an era called Shōwa. I do not remember having been born in that era at all. That means that this birth date is probably not mine at all. Next to my birth date there is a picture. There is a girl who looks a little bit like me, though she is quite different from me. The length of her hair and its style are different from mine. The expression on her face. That is not the way I smile. I don't smile like that at all. I rarely smile at all. It is not my face at all. It is not my I.D. card.

Kita Kyushu Kirigaoka Municipal Junior High. I have never heard of such a place. I don't remember ever going to that junior high school. Toshiko Hirata. 4th class in the 9th grade. I am not familiar with such a name. It is not my name. It is not my I.D. Or if it is, the person here is not me at all.

kiyoko horiba

IN MEMORY OF THE WATER GODDESS

Once upon a time
there was an Inuit maiden named Sedona
her elegant body swathed
in an anorak of a polar bear's white skin
carrying a bow and arrows under her arm
riding a sled pulled by dogs
as if flying on the shiny light blue field of ice
chased by many suitors
no one could catch her
she turned them all away
so her father cursed her pride and wed her to his dog
she was tricked into marrying a gull
it held her in its bill
flapped its wings
and flew to its nest on the far ice field
dropping her
into the sea.

Her father rescued her in his kayak
but the bird stirred up a storm
to overturn the kayak
in terror the father threw his daughter
into the sea.

Sedona cried, holding onto the edge of the kayak
but her father cut off all her fingers
scattering them in the water where they became seals, whales
walruses, right-eyed flounders, herring and salmon
snails and hundreds of tiny fish
all life
in the sea.

Through the shimmering buoyant dance of life
Sedona swayed as she fell to the depths of the sea
transformed into a mermaid
by the time she sat on the algae-covered throne
she had become the ruler of the sea,
the Goddess.

Day and night fish sprout
from her fingerless hands
from her scales and fins
they'll grow for eternity
but when the shadow of the kayak
floats overhead

how she yearns
and raises her hands high above her head
the fish flow out from her wounds
to follow the kayak home

> a goddess of all life
> giving nourishment to everything
> Goddess Sedona
> holding life both in the sea and on land
> in her wounded hands

oh, the breasts of the nurturing sea

THE TAIL TRIBE

Born under the poor thatched roof
on the Ryukyu Islands
then sold again

suffering a *gachimaya*'s* hunger
they studied the snakeskin shamisen and danced
powdering their necks with white talc
finding a patron was the only way to live
for the women called Ju Ri,†
the "tail tribe"

those two letters
knock the wind out of me

but the playful letters signifying four legs
are said to be mere phonetic equivalents
then that's all the more reason
beautiful characters should have been chosen

the Ju Ri set up their "families" with affection
and remained loyal to their patrons
who still praise them now

and yet on the islands
where women were called Bi Rui
where men who called them that
felt nothing of their pain
they still live together

but an infinite loneliness
dampens each house
like the early summer rain.

noriko ibaragi

WHEN I WAS AT MY MOST BEAUTIFUL

When I was at my most beautiful
town after town came crashing down.
I caught glimpses of the blue sky
from the most unexpected places.

When I was at my most beautiful
people were dying all around me
in factories, at sea, on islands without names
I lost my chance to make the best of myself.

When I was at my most beautiful
none of the young men brought me tender gifts
all they knew how to do was salute
and set out for war, leaving only their glances behind.

When I was at my most beautiful
my head was empty

my mind obstinate
but my arms and legs shone like chestnuts.

When I was at my most beautiful
my country lost the war
how could all that have happened?
I rolled up my sleeves and marched around my humiliated
    town.

When I was at my most beautiful
jazz flowed from the radio
I devoured the sweet exotic sounds
the way I smoked my first forbidden cigarettes.

When I was at my most beautiful
I was so very unhappy
I was so very awkward
and so terribly lonely.

So I decided I'd live a very long time
Like old man Rouault
who painted his most beautiful works in his old age
                        if I could.

LULLABY FOR A GIANT

Goodnight, giant.
Why are you wide awake at night
doing what rare birds do?
Close your eyelids, let your mouth fall open
as if you were dead.
At night when birds and trees are asleep
you alone remain awake, eyes wide—
I don't know what you're doing.

This progress that makes your heart's rivers groan
something is wrong with it
something is terribly wrong.

What has true value is hard to come by
what has true value is hard to come by
not to say that everything you've done
is worthless, but . . .

Sleep well, giant.
Follow me to a dark forest in the distance
where a cold fountain spouts something that glistens,
running down from the mountains.
Surely you can fill a pail with springwater
just don't ask what it is.

Goodnight, giant.
Make sure to fill a pail
or you'll certainly run dry.
Sleep well, giant.
Somewhere there's a quiet place
we both can go.
I will follow you there.

JUNE

Is there a beautiful village left anywhere?
After a day's work, drinking dark beer
laying down baskets, putting hoes to rest
men and women tipping back their full glasses.

Is there a beautiful village left anywhere?
Fruit trees lining the street endlessly
violet twilight overflowing
with the tender murmurs of the young.

Is there force left among beautiful people anywhere
Living together in the same age?
Intimacy, fascination, then anger as
Strong forces begin to emerge.

yohko isaka

SMOKING LESSONS

Since the Kamakura Period*
women have clung to their lovers
saying *don't throw me away*—
today in a certain Tokyo cafe
I face my lover
whose pleading eyes
make me see double.
I just say
I'd never throw a man out like a scrap of paper
besides, you shouldn't talk that way
then I do what men
have always done
and pull out a cigarette,
thinking *I'm in the right*
I won't give in
and blow out
the flame.

WEEKDAY DUCKS

We ate potstickers
with a visiting friend
our noisy chewing made us notice
his lonely single life
peeling our backs off from the shabby
folding chairs, we watched a night
baseball game together

The ballpark was
systematically controlled
preventing unnecessary risk
the field divided
into diamond shapes.
A hardball went outfield
the field's surface stayed silent
each angle tightening its reins.

At night when the half-warm sperm
sink beside the egg
we can't see the light
of a falling white
ball, a
falling nuclear
missile
so we just give each other

these floating potstickers.
I should go now
is what he says
and I put my
red lipstick on
to see him off,
this man who has no job.

On our way, in the park
the man squats with the night ducks
from the pond and speaks to them, pulling me in
from the distance where I stand, jerking me
by the hand.
I lean back, not wanting to get
my red lipstick on him
not wanting to give in that much.
As for the man,
why does he pull me
(someone he doesn't even love)
by the hand?
The cliff of his cheeks
illuminated amidst the trees
old age seems somehow
older still, and love surfaces oily
on my face.

The two of us like ducks
standing Deva Kings,
our brains buried in earth and sand.
Vinegar running wet down the man's chest
my homemade cooking vomited up with sake
indistinguishable in the bright and dark
sides of nightfall
bamboo!
bamboo poles!
bamboo!
bamboo poles!
why is the streetseller singing
so late at night?

Covering over the waves
being swept up by the waves
each month I grow fatter.
The brown bank where the man and I walked
is now covered in scaffolding
splitting into the earth's seismic waves.

At the swaying sidewalk stand
I bought a soft ice cream cone
and ate it standing up,
stabbing at its soft blandness
with my tongue.

rin ishigaki

ISLAND

I'm standing in a full-length mirror.
A lone,
small island
isolated from everyone.

I know
the island's history
and size,
its waist and bust and hips,
and clothing, which changes by season.

The call of its birds
its hidden spring
the smell of flowers.

I
live on this island.

I've tended it and made it grow.
Yet,
it's impossible to really know this island
impossible too,
to stay here.

In a full-length mirror
I'm staring at
myself
a far-off island.

THE LOAD

When I carried a load
a force was set in motion
      "it will fall."

At the dangerous edge, the precipice of the sky
the earth was kind enough
to hold
it back.

So it was heavy
to us
always
love was.

THREE FISH

A tropical fish died.
It sank
on its little white belly.

A fish came up
and poked the tip of its mouth
but its expression didn't change.

Another came up and poked it
for a very long time
only to eat it in the end.

This is justice.
If there's anything
more right than this
said the fish,
rising to the water's surface,

name it.

WHEN I WAS AT MY MOST BEAUTIFUL

WATASHI GA ICHIBAN KIREI DATTA TOKI

watashi ga ichiban kirei datta toki
machimachi wa garagara kuzurete itte
tondemonai tokoro kara
aozora nanka ga mietari shita

watashi ga ichiban kirei datta toki
mawari no hitotachi ga takusan shinda
kōjō de umi de namonai shima de
watashi wa oshare no kikkake o otoshite shimatta

watashi ga ichiban kirei datta toki
dare mo yasashii okurimono o sasagete wa kurenakatta
otokotachi wa kyoshu no rei shika shiranakute
kirei na manazashi dake o nokoshi mina tatte itta

watashi ga ichiban kirei datta toki
watashi no atama wa karappo de
watashi no kokoro wa kataku na de
te ashi bakari ga kuri iro ni hikatta

watashi ga ichiban kirei datta toki
watashi no kuni wa sensō de maketa
sonna baka na koto-tte aru mono ka
burausu no ude o makuri hikutsu na machi o noshi aruita

watashi ga ichiban kirei datta toki
rajio kara wa jazu ga afureta
kin'en o yabutta toki no yō ni kurakura shinagara
watashi wa ikoku no amai ongaku o musabotta

わたしが一番きれいだったとき

わたしが一番きれいだったとき
街々はがらがら崩れていって
とんでもないところから
青空なんかが見えたりした

わたしが一番きれいだったとき
まわりの人達が沢山死んだ
工場で　海で　名もない島で
わたしはおしゃれのきっかけを落してしまった

わたしが一番きれいだったとき
だれもやさしい贈物を捧げてはくれなかった
男たちは挙手の礼しか知らなくて
きれいな眼差だけを残し皆発っていった

わたしが一番きれいだったとき
わたしの頭はからっぽで
わたしの心はかたくなで
手足ばかりが栗色に光った

わたしが一番きれいだったとき
わたしの国は戦争で負けた
そんな馬鹿なことってあるものか
ブラウスの腕をまくり卑屈な町をのし歩いた

わたしが一番きれいだったとき
ラジオからはジャズが溢れた
禁煙を破ったときのようにくらくらしながら
わたしは異国の甘い音楽をむさぼった

watashi ga ichiban kirei datta toki
watashi wa totemo fushiawase
watashi wa totemo tonchinkan
watashi wa meppō sabishikatta

dakara kimeta dekireba nagaiki suru koto ni
toshi totte kara sugoku utsukushii e o kaita
furansu no Ruō jii-san no yō ni
ne

わたしが一番きれいだったとき
わたしはとてもふしあわせ
わたしはとてもとんちんかん
わたしはめっぽうさびしかった

だから決めた　できれば長生きすることに
年とってから凄く美しい絵を描いた
フランスのルオー爺さんのように
　　　　　　　　　　　　　　　ね

hiromi itō

HARAKIRI

Cherry blossoms are falling
I once met a *harakiri* fanatic named Mr. O
And asked him "Who would you like to see commit *harakiri*
Among all the famous actors in Japan?"
And Mr. O said,
"Well, I've never thought about it . . . "
Then he folded his arms across his chest,
Looked up and groaned.
"Ummmm . . . " he said,
"I guess it would have to be Masaya Oki.*
He jumped off the Keio Plaza Hotel.
I liked the expression on his face before he died,
So I can easily imagine him committing *harakiri*."

"How would you make him do it?" I asked, picturing him
Disemboweling himself in the clean white robes of Asano
    Takumi no Kami.†

"He'd have to be naked. He'd have to do it
Standing up," said Mr. O.
"Where would you make him do it?"
"Ummmm . . . ," he said,
"It must be in a graveyard.
The graveyard where the
Cherry blossoms are falling."

Cherry blossoms are falling

"Do you mean he is
Totally naked under his robe?"
"No, he should wear a loincloth
Tight around his penis,
Covering every erogenous zone
From the penis to the perineum to the asshole."

Cherry blossoms are falling

Random stupas line the graveyards

ha ha

"It's a little kinky,
But it will do."

"Will Masaya Oki die in great pain, or . . . ?" I asked.
"Yes, he should suffer. He should be in agony for a long
    time.
Then he will die and become my double," said Mr. O
Who wore a tight white loincloth,
Stood up and disemboweled himself.
Harakiri should be beautiful, he thinks.

After all, it is the male aesthetic.
He thinks it should be cherry blossoms
He thinks it should be cherry blossoms
In full bloom
He thinks cherry blossoms in full bloom
Should fall
He wants to die while he is
Still beautiful
He will be sixty in a few years
He thinks *harakiri* is Asano Takumi no Kami
He thinks Yukio Mishima beat him to it.
He thinks graveyards should have stupas
He thinks *harakiri* should be committed
Under the cherry blossoms
                              ha ha
"I know, it's kind of sick," he said.
He thinks *bushido* should have cherry blossoms
He thinks samurai are always
Looking for a place to die.
I failed to hear
If his ancestors were samurai.

He thinks pain will become pleasure
If he trains himself
"That's why I'm training myself now," he says,
        (masturbating)
I'm sure it's extremely exciting

To commit *harakiri* facing a woman
Mr. O says,
    (masturbating)
samurai
    (masturbating)
ha ha
    (masturbating)
cherry blossoms
    (masturbating)
falling
    (masturbating)
It's really kind of kinky.

THE COYOTE

i.

My grandmother was a medium
My mother was a sorcerer
One aunt was a geisha
Another had tuberculosis
Still another was barren
All were beautiful
And knew the magical rite
My mother taught me
With sake, rice, and salt

We lived in fear of snakes, water
& the East.

ii.
My two-month-old daughter
Just started talking
The coyote speaks to her
When it speaks she just smiles
On and on and on
When the coyote says *a dry plain*
My daughter says *plain plain plain*
If the coyote says *she doesn't lie*
My daughter says *don't don't don't*
The coyote says *I'm hungry*
My daughter says *I'm hungry too*
When the coyote laughs
My daughter says *huh-ugh*

My daughter's father said:
> *I want to concentrate on the coyote. I want to isolate myself.*
> *See nothing other than the coyote.*
>> *I want to be the coyote.**
My own father said the same thing.

iii.
My mother had plenty of milk
Too much to feed just one daughter
My grandmother also had plenty of milk

She gave birth to four girls and two boys
Brought them all up and fed them all
One aunt had plenty of milk as well
Another gave birth to three boys,
Brought them all up and fed them all
And another aunt gave her dry breast
To her adopted child & let the child suck until
Milk came like so much rain.

iv.
Everything is wet.
The smiling face of my grandmother is
Damp in its frame
Eyebrowless, toothless
The beautiful face of my aunt is
Thick-lipped, lacking chin, teeth, or hair
The beautiful face of another aunt is
Eyebrows wasted down to nothing
The beautiful face of another aunt
Spotted with age
The beautiful face of my mother
Cheeks and eyes slanting
Without hair in her armpits
Without teeth
All of their breasts sagged.

v.

They gather in a circle,
Bouncing the family babies
My daughter is the only granddaughter
The only niece
The women in the circle speak
Their words becoming baby talk
Instantaneously
From fifty to ninety
(Though the eldest has been dead 10 years)
Come into the circle
& chant *gate gate paragate*
parasamagate
bodhi swaha
gate gate paaraagate parasamagate
*gate gate paaraagate paraparagate gagagate paragate**

vi.

My grandmother was a medium
My mother was a sorcerer
One aunt was a geisha
Another had tuberculosis
One was barren
My grandfather was paralyzed
My uncle died young.

Another was dumb as an oyster
& my father is unrelated

To any of them.
My mother's husband turned away from her
& before I gave birth
To my daughter, so did mine.

The coyote says:
gate gate paragate
My daughter says *parasamagate*
The coyote says *bodhi swaha*
My daughter says *gate gate paaraagate parasamagate*
gate gate paaraagate paraparagate gagagate paragate

vii.
It's so humid
This time of year
& raining.
My mother curses
The humidity
Calling out an incantation
Sake and rain!
Rice and rain!
Salt and rain!

My Lord
Master snake
Forgive us—
Let the water flow eastward!

KILLING KANOKO

"That is a leg. To determine the size of the fetus, measure
   one of the limbs. Fifteen weeks is correct."
"About three centimeters. A torn-off thigh, knees, calves,
   feet, five toes."
"Two fetuses were born alive in one week. All the women on
   this floor are trying to somehow suppress the feeling
   they have when they have abortions, and it was a disaster
   when the babies cried!"

I was reading a book
When my sister said
She "got rid of a little devil in her tummy"
To use her words.
I got rid of a little devil in my tummy
Congratulations.
My daughter Kanoko was not gotten rid of
But my sister asked if I'd ever done "it"
And I answered yes,
But getting rid of a little devil in my tummy
Would not be my choice of words.
Kanoko was not gotten rid of
But I terminated the pregnancy
Of a fetus that must have resembled her.
The fetus that must have resembled her
Might have grown and I might have

Had a baby that greatly resembled Kanoko
But is not Kanoko
Congratulations on the destruction
Congratulations on the destruction
Congratulations on the destruction
When I had a D&C the doctor said,
"Because your baby is big, you'll have plenty of milk"
But I just laughed it off
Ha Ha
Ha Ha
Actually he was right
I had plenty of milk
When I squeezed my breasts
It stained my clothes.
My breasts didn't swell or itch or anything
But you couldn't exactly say
They were beautiful.
Congratulations.
Anyway,
It's good to have milk,
Something comforting and sweet
Springing from nowhere.
It's good to have milk
Because I secrete something like milk
Sold at the grocery store
Because I secrete it

Like piss spit tears and discharge
Because plenty of milk
Flows from my breasts,
And something like milk gushes out of
My ass, mouth, and vagina
It makes me so very happy
Congratulations.
I had the abortion
During the middle of my second trimester
I asked the doctor what sex the baby was,
But "baby" is inaccurate
It's really just a fetus.
Of course, the doctor won't say,
Because the shock is too much
On the mother's body.
But this mother's body wonders
Whether it was a boy or girl
That resembled Kanoko.
When I was pregnant
I had toxemia
I had a cyst full of water
I saw all the lumps that filled my uterus,
They too must have resembled Kanoko
I had uterine cancer
I had a hysterectomy,
They even took my ovaries out.

I had enforced labor & slow contractions
I had an episiotomy.
My uterus was swollen
My body was full
I could eat as much as I wanted
And masturbate endlessly.
Ahhh, the happy fingers of the pregnant woman,
Imagining the moment of her baby's birth.
You could say I was happily pregnant.
That's why I gave my breasts to my baby.
Congratulations on the destruction.
Now Kanoko is six months old
Her teeth are growing
Wanting to bite my nipples off,
Waiting for her chance.
Kanoko ate my time away
Robbed me of sustenance
Threatened my appetite
Pulled out my hair & forced me to change her dirty diapers.
I want to desert her
I want to desert dirty Kanoko
I want to desert Kanoko who bites my nipples
Before she sheds any more of my blood
I want to desert her or kill her.
I myself have committed infanticide
I've disposed of the corpse

It's easy right after the delivery,
Easier than an abortion if you don't get caught.
I'm sure I could do it again
Without getting caught.
I can easily bury Kanoko
Congratulations on the buried Kanokos
Congratulations
We must be fruitful and multiply
We must conceive one Kanoko after another
Then we must weed out all of them
Except one
The Kanoko of the moment
Who bites my nipples.
Congratulations on the destruction
Congratulations on the destruction
Congratulations on the destruction
Congratulations on the destruction
Congratulations on the destruction
Congratulations on the destruction
It's fun to whip the stepchild
It's fun to kill the stepchild
(I've done it myself)
But my own child is more lovable.
It's a pleasure to abandon a child
(I've done it)
I'm more lovable.

Congratulations
Congratulations on the destruction
Congratulations.
Everyone congratulated me
Gen-ichirō gave me a bottle of Medoc
Higuchi roses
Kōhei sent me a stuffed rabbit
Ishizeki a bear
Miyashita delivered a diaper bag
Shiroyasu a papier-mâché dog
Abe and Iwasaki handed me money
Non baked me a cake
Kaneko bought me a video camera
Kosaki sent me a telegram
Everone congratulated me
Thank you, thank you.
While happy Kanoko bites my nipples
Congratulations
Congratulations
How great it would be
To abandon her
Gloomy, with a guilty conscience,
I want to leave her in Tokyo
Desert her deliriously.
Congratulations
Congratulations on the destruction

Congratulations on the destruction
Teruko—
      Congratulations on your abortion
Mihoko—
      Congratulations on deserting little Take
Kumiko—
      Congratulations on killing Tomo,
Mari—
      Why don't you leave little Nonoho behind?
Mayumi—
      Was your fetus male or female?
Sweet Riko—
      Isn't it about time you got rid of Kota?

Let's all desert the daughters and sons
Who grind their teeth and bite our nipples.

My friend Hiromi
Leapt to her death three years ago today
Reportedly due to "man trouble"
But she was known to have had "athlete's foot."
That's why she hid her athlete's foot in her socks,
Put on her jeans and leapt.
The dead two legs and belly
Of the twenty-four-year-old
Strangely beautiful woman—
I can't get them out of my head

Even after three years,
Though I didn't actually see them
On the ground.
Two legs and belly of the dead
Two legs and belly of the dead
Congratulations on the destruction.

Once I suddenly got furious at Kanoko
And hit her on the head with an alarm clock
Next to my hand.
She fell down and didn't move at all.
I yelled at her and shook her,
I slapped her but she didn't move.
I was terrified at the thought
That I had killed her
So I deserted her body and went out.
When I came back two hours later
She still looked dead,
And black ants swarmed
All over her body.
Still, she seemed to have shifted a little
From where she'd been when I'd left her.

Then I found a baby sparrow
Struggling on the hot street,
Picked it up and moved it
To a wet corner of the edge of the road.

Better, I thought,
Than the dry side of the road.
But still, the road was a road,
Still dangerous,
With nowhere to hide.
So I moved it again to a grassy spot
And checked on it on my way back home.

Congratulations on the destruction
I noticed the swarm of ants
In the neighborhood
But didn't make the connection
At first, ants were everywhere on the baby sparrow
Except on its head.
Now they swarmed to its head while
It moved its featherless wings,
Straining to escape.
I tried to get away from the ants
All over its body.

Congratulations on the destruction
Congratulations on the destruction
I was able to touch the pure baby sparrow
But I couldn't touch the one covered with ants
I ran away,
Thinking of how I'd deserted Kanoko
Covered with ants.

Still, I'm not afraid of Kanoko—
It's the ants I'm afraid of.
Congratulations on the destruction
Congratulations on the destruction
Congratulations on the destruction
Congratulations on the destruction.

yuri kageyama

POETIC GAMESMANSHIP

Words at their disposal like Kleenex
The millions of white *tanzaku* strips
Scribbled with allusions,
Seasonally correct,
Backwards and forwards from the *saijiki* text*

    As spring arouses
    Curled, a damp antenna-less snail,
    My son's soft penis

Count the rhythms, five-seven-five
The haiku masters
With their Mishima haircuts
Flex their poetic muscle
Here at the haiku meet

Like raw raspberries
His firm hand reaches to peel
My hardened nipples

"*Umai—jitsuni umai—**
The repetition of the 'i' sound
The unexpected absurdity of the first phrase—
Brilliant!"

As men live and women die
As menstrual blood spurts from the wounds of war
As time turns and the globe groans
"*Umai, jitsuni umai!*"

Maggots mixed with rice
I don't want to talk with you
In the kitchen

All
Caught in the dignified accident of frog-leaping
Moments
Scored on points of polite camaraderie
But no one cries or really laughs

Haiku is to poetry
What Hanayagi† dance is
To freaking out, wild, baby, hiphopping on the disco floor

An old wooden desk
Yellow dots of light, shrieking
Filling Van Gogh's room.

FOX SPIRITS: UPON VISITING
THE TOYOKAWA INARI SHRINE

Beneath the stone *torii* gate
my son prays to the Fox spirit
for money to buy his computer games
frozen in their haughty statue sneers
tails erect
their ears sometimes chipped
granite-engraved whiskers
the shock of a scarlet bib
they only cough
kon-kon-kon
when backs are turned.

The vendor with wrinkled hands
her stall lined with rows of purses
fox-shaped charms promising wealth
says the conniving Fox
helps merchants thrive
the people clap their hands to awaken the Gods

throwing in yen with a clatter
as reminders of what they want
they turn down that dirt path
where flapping flags on both sides
boast rich donors' names painted in red.

Then a sudden circular clearing of moss
covered from end to end with
foxes
of all sizes and expressions, hundreds
caught in perpetual mid-motion.

The bestial spirits are everywhere
in wells, the threshold
the air you breathe
if you don't watch out, they'll possess you
sit right on your shoulder
where you can't see them
like gray whispering clouds.

You'll turn out like that village widow
gorging herself
looking up from the paulowania rice bin
no guilt on her face
spotted with fluffy grain
like unforgiving pockmarks.

HOMECOMING II

The pottery brought back from Hagi
has khaki spottles on pale pink glaze
it still looks beautiful holding

tossed salad or vanilla gelato.
The silver-green teapot is
a perfect sugar bowl, the spout nestling

the spoon, the lid fitting just right—
though in Japan, you must remember to
use each vessel correctly

the rice bowl on the left with its spouse
miso soup in wooden lacquer to the right,
the chopsticks resting their narrow

ends on a porcelain knot—
tanned children in crisp summer kimonos
their mosquito-bitten legs tripping over their sandals

follow the *taiko* drums drifting with the
smell of roasting dinner mackerel
to nearby shrines

where bobbing yoyo balloons filled with water
wait to be fished, and ginger ale
bottles the same color as their stopper marbles inside

will spurt frothy soda when they get pushed
in, clinking against the glass
when you drink.

Your parents have forgiven you:
like a good Japanese daughter
you have born a son

See, he has a blue yoyo hanging from his finger
and points to a mask of a comic-book superhero
and pleads already in Japanese.

This country, thousands upon thousands of years old
stone turning to rock until
covered with the moss of Kyoto temples—

Take your boy to this land, where
Genji and Heike* fireflies take flight
in a storm of starlight.

Return
I promise you, and
you will never have to leave again.

ritsuko kawabata

THE INCARNATION

Coral islands
Floating flat and green
In the South Pacific
The pure white sandy beaches of Ottakai*
Layered cobalt and milk
The colors of the sea.

"The island seems to have gotten bigger"
One survivor murmurs.
A party of six has landed
On a road running from east to west
Through the island's center.
The Japanese Army walked this road
My husband must have walked there too
I am thinking
As I follow this way now.

On both sides of the road
Palm trees grow thick, shutting out the sky
Though the soil looks poor
The trees stand tall and manly.

The palm leaves sway
Trying to tell me something
(They must be the incarnations of our
Husbands!)
Many soldiers turned to dust
    on this island
During the war.

Forty-five years have gone by since then
At the base of the palms
There used to be a barracks
I put up a *dagoba**
Lighting incense
And offering cherry blossoms
Sake, cigarettes, and rice
To the spirits of the dead.

Why?
For what?
Those men who were brought here from afar
Traveling three thousand miles by sea
    in forty days

Only to live just ten months after landing
My husband died for nothing.

Oh, gentle palm
That you might
Use my tears that soak the earth,
Gentle palm.

OLDER SISTER, YOUNGER SISTER

To me, my younger sister seemed
Like my child
Like a god
Smiling softly
While I prepared our meals
And set them in front of her.
Before eating, she'd say *thank you*
When she finished, *thank you*
Was said again.

I was a farmer
I worked and shopped
I washed and cooked
Then said to my sister
     Dinner's ready

Sometimes,
I'd stop to wonder
Why I had to take care of her

But then again—

My weak sister's role was to be supported
My role as the stronger was to support
Both of us protected by

God's love,
Buddha's mercy
The wise providence of heaven.

SISTERS

The younger sister who fell ill during the war
The elder who lost her husband
Lived like mother and daughter
Long before they knew it.

Ten years ago
We buried our parents
In Kamakura
Together

Now I'm going to the graveyard
Again
With my little sister,

Her ashes
against my breast.

iro kitadai

THE SUNSET WAS MORE BEAUTIFUL AFTER I LEARNED HOW TO WRITE KANA

Because my family was poor, I didn't go to school.
So I didn't know how to write *kana*.
I'm learning in an education class against illiteracy
I've learned almost all of them.

I used to ask the receptionist to write my name
at the doctor's office, but now I try to write it myself.
The nurse calls out, "Ms. Kitadai," which makes me very
    happy.
Until now, the sunset wasn't that beautiful.
But now, after having learned how to write *kana*
I think they're so beautiful.

I try to pay attention to street signs,
walking on the street,

I'm excited to find the characters
I've learned.
Because I've learned numbers,
I enjoy going to supermarkets
and the Thursday market,
and I don't have to humiliate myself
because I now can figure out
my room number in a hotel.
I'm going to study even harder from now on.
I wish I had ten years more to live.

masayo koike

APPLE

And so,
this morning i put an apple
on my palm

its weight was very erotic
and shot straight down to the tip of my toes
it's no wonder that the center of the earth
is being pulled toward me, inch by inch
on this heavy and powerful morning

through the slightly open window
freshly squeezed houses come spilling in by rows
somewhere i hear ten transparent fingers
flipping through the pages of a new dictionary
daringly, physically
wanting to know what i'm feeling
makes me feel fresh

on this kind of morning
when an apple on my palm
becomes an extension of me

it weighs as much as the feelings
i've lost

i won't see him anymore
and so
this morning i put an apple
on my palm.

MY LITTLE SISTER IS MISSING

I call the swaying body
my gentle little sister
she has a lightness
that has never weighed her down

in still-wet jeans
she walks on a newly sewn field
beautiful barefoot July

enraptured,
that's the place where
I lost sight of her heels.

Catching the summer coastline at my eyebrow's edge
leaving the raindrops behind at my temples.

Since then,
my little sister has been missing.

Waves searching for an island
swaying in an empty bottle.

The market of wind
begins here.

Drowning in grass waves
a one-legged wooden chair
gracefully
takes on the blue sky.

COMPOSITION

After only one child's name
has been called from a picture
a bright classroom,
a pupil who has been absent for a long time

(closing a book)

after leaving a little bird by the window
where has that child gone
leaving behind a new shadow?

the sun has slowly gone down
during the day
the seats next to the window are warm

in the evening classroom,
from where everyone has gone
the blackboard quietly grows cold

When the town I grew up in is praised
it's as if someone is washing my feet

(an untitled composition pinned to the wall)

THE JUDGE'S NECK

Bumping into the judge
in the packed elevator—
a thick neck
bordered by a neat shirt
the clean, smooth neck
blocking my way—

Yeah, I know
you're judging others
with this neck—
a pillar of importance
for looking straight down all the time
from a high place.
That's why
I'd like to embrace you
and suck your neck
(it's gotten so big)
and from its base
I'd like to shake you.

The weather is nice today
outside the District Court.
What went down to the ninth floor
and walked away to the courtroom
is a back in a business suit
whose eyes and mouth
I'm not familiar with.
But what I'm all too familiar with
is the afternoon neck

—sitting
      in such a dignified manner—
of the judge
in April.

APPLE

RINGO

tokoro de
kyō no asa wa
ringo o hitotsu te no hira e noseta

tsumasaki made kichin to todokerarete iku
kore wa totemo erochikku na omosa da
chikyū no chūshin ga ima koko e
jirijiri to zurasarete mo fushigi wa nai
sonna iryoku no aru kono asa no katamari de aru

usuku aita mado kara
shiboritate no machinami ga koborete kuru to
dokoka de totemo tōmei na jusshi ga
atarashii jisho o mekuru oto
omoikiri yoku butsuriteki ni
tonde mo nai hodo sugasugashiku
watashi no kimochi o sokuryō shitai
sonna asa
ringo wa hitotsu te no hira no ue
watashi wa ringo no tsuzuki ni naru

nakunatta kimochibun kurai no omosa ka

ano hito to mō awanai
sōshite
kyō no asa wa
ringo o hitotsu te no hira e noseta

りんご

ところで
きょうのあさは
りんごをひとつ　てのひらへのせた

つま先まで　きちんと届けられていく
これはとてもエロティックなおもさだ
地球の中心が　いまここへ
じりじりとずらされても不思議はない
そんな威力のある、　このあさのかたまりである

うすくあいた窓から
しぼりたての町並がこぼれてくる　と
どこかで　とてもとうめいな十指が
あたらしい辞書をめくるおと
おもいきりよく物理的に
とんでもないほどすがすがしく
わたしのきもちをそくりょうしたい
そんなあさ
りんごはひとつ　てのひらのうえ
わたしはりんごのつづきになる

なくなったきもち分くらいのおもさ　か

あのひとと　もう会わない
そうして
きょうのあさは
りんごをひとつ　てのひらへのせた

rumiko kōra

TREE

Within a tree
there is another tree that does not yet exist
now its branches tremble in the wind.

Within the blue sky
there is another blue sky that does not yet exist
now a bird flies across its horizon.

Within a body
there is another body that does not yet exist
now its shrine gathers new blood.

Within a city
there is another city that does not yet exist
now its plazas sway where I am heading.

BENEATH THE EARTH

On the invisible earth
The sound of dead leaves brushing against each other
Cuts to my heart, a dappled sorrow
Flowing into the sky.

The fur of a small dog playing on a winter day
Shining with short-tempered hunger
The ground rearing up, throwing out
Toads, old gekkos in vain.

A forgotten footstool, a gardener's tool
The old stuck windowpane
A wind resurrecting footsteps
Buried beneath cracked cobblestones.

The sky, separated from me by varying shades of blue
Descends on me
With a cruel unknown hope
And clear scornful laughter.

The eyes of the blue sky bore into me
The cunning earth, the fertile mother
This hollow heart a scar of my desire
For you.

VASE

red copper vase in the shape of a bud
no flowers blooming from it now
but the clear clear crimson
is the color of daybreak
the color of slightly opened lips
its graceful, curvy shape
the blazing form
of a naked body

(oh, why do people
risk such violent hope
on a future full of obstacles
while lavishing flowers
on healthy souls?)

red copper vase
radiating the color of daybreak
inside it
the darkness deepens
with visions
and ruin

SPROUT

When I discovered
that the Japanese for "sprout"
was written with "crown of grass" on top of "tusk"
I imagined a sprout appearing from the ground
breaking through the frozen air.

Men of old must have gotten discouraged
roaming the mountains all day long
not finding a single wild boar or deer
no doubt they'd hunted them all down
a family can't live on rabbits and birds alone.

They must have seen a field one day
where women were growing potatoes,
with its rows of curved sprouts
gleaming like polished white tusks.

"These are our tusks," they must have thought
so they made the character for "sprout"
with a crown of grass atop a tusk
and declared the sprouts were theirs
because those who make the words rule the world.

In a woman's illusory field
invisible sprouts keep

breaking through the frozen earth
their fresh tusks appearing from the ground
not to tear, but to yield.

teruko kunimine

MR. LABYRINTH'S TANK

Mr. Labyrinth's residence is a huge fish tank that sank to the
    depths of the sea
Mr. Labyrinth's living room is a transparent secret room
    hanging in the tank
Mr. Labyrinth's garden is heaven for jellyfish who have no
    enemies
Mr. Labyrinth is a secret collector of jellyfish
Mr. Labyrinth yearns for a new species of jellyfish
Mr. Labyrinth takes walks in the coral garden in the early
    morning

    swaying about
        floating around

The purple jellyfish is a windbell who has wet dreams
The straw-hat-with-flowers on it jellyfish is a prism of the
    sea   The sun jellyfish is the thinnest mystery

The multi-legged jellyfish is an unattainable tremolo
The one-legged jellyfish is a question mark in the saltwater
The oberia jellyfish is a soul that slipped away before
    knowledge

             swaying about
    floating around

Mr. Labyrinth studies the coolness of gelatinous matter
Mr. Labyrinth studies the colors of the jellyfish
Mr. Labyrinth studies the poison of nettles
Mr. Labyrinth studies the openings and closings of
    umbrellas
Mr. Labyrinth studies the reflection of bright eyespots
Mr. Labyrinth studies the joys of jellyfish

       swaying about
                      floating around

Mr. Labyrinth discovered the reason a jellyfish is a jellyfish
About a minute before the jellyfish found out why a man is a
    man
A solemn burial was held at sea
of Mr. Labyrinth's study notes and body
Nothing remained

        swaying about
    floating around

"Life in nature knows no rest"
Jellyfish pretend to go crazy
Looking up at Yonaguni Island from the depths of the clear
    blue sea
The blue blue sky
A looking glass reflecting the jellyfish

Swaying about
        floating around
                in
                        the water tank
            now
                now
                    now
                            now

    now.

DAY OF OBSCENITY

There are some days when every relationship feels obscene.
On the day it rained a funeral was held, and it was Monday.
The garish gold limousine making its grand gesture under
the wet cherry blossoms in the crematorium on top of the
steep slope was an artificial obscenity. Natural obscenity
pushes open a gap in the gravel when rain falls and sinks
into it. The eyes that peered one after another through the

window of the coffin saying their final farewells were pious obscenity, and the iron gate through which the coffin entered the incinerator was casually obscene, smooth as the entrance to a love hotel.

The white handkerchiefs of the ones who cry, the one who consoles, the one who endures, and the one with a strong sense of duty were opened, grasped, and folded again obscenely. Going down the mountain there was a roadside vending machine selling porno magazines, the only thing that looked innocent and clean and pure.

Relationship, relationship rolls on my tongue, not able to be vomited out or crushed between my teeth. I return home acting casual but the relationship between a husband, his wife, and their children is shamelessly advertised from the red mailbox on the gate of the small home of this obscene family.

kiyoko nagase

TO THE ONE WHO COMES AT DAYBREAK

To the one who comes at daybreak
The one who comes silently, softly
From where a dove cries:
The ups and downs of life have been steep beyond compare.
Now I am old,
And just like other people who have passed their years
I yearn for the days of my youth ten million times over.

Back then, when I ran away from home
Taking only a small wicker basket
My legs trembled in the air.
I didn't know myself where to go
And listened only to my heart in love.
Youth—it was such stifling agony.

If only you had come then!
How eagerly I waited for you.

Should I have told a roadside willow?
Should I have asked the swirling wind?
You were too far away to hear.
And like the whistle of a train disappearing into the glowing
    dawn
You too disappeared.

Now everything has left me
Even if you came today, it would be too late
My whole life has already passed by, but still
To the one who comes at daybreak
The one who comes silently, softly
The one whose steps are silent,
You're the one
For whom I cry.

IS GETTING OLD ROMANTIC?

Is getting old romantic?
since there is so little time left
my mind rushes morning and night
like walking the narrow ledge
at the tip of a precipice

Oh, now I know the thrills of these lives of ours
and yet, when I go outside in the winter light

though my walk is unsteady
I can't explain what still holds me up
at dusk the moon and Venus seem to shed soft light
upon my body only.

This morning when I tried to pick leeks for morning soup
my fingers felt chilled, I felt the frost.
Still, the sun's blue rays spread
and I couldn't open my eyes
in spite of myself,
I fell
towards spring.

THE CIRCLE DANCE

Among the pretty girls
my daughter is dancing, too.
Hidden by the crowd
I stare at her.
The poppy-colored *obi* I tied
seems too stiff, too new for her kimono
moving her body shyly
she dances among her girlfriends.
Doesn't she look as good as the others?
Does she look happy?
Having always kept her close at home

I've never watched her from a distance.
I wonder if she cherishes
the wishes and dreams I would have
At her age?
Is someone else watching her too?
The dancer's circle is slowly opening out,
the voices of song are rising.
The evening moon has left the mountain
and the sky is covered with rippling clouds.
In every ripple, silver beams begin to shine.
Stepping forward softly, then retreating
blurred like a large flower in a blue haze
is a group of fairies in a lake
each one indistinguishable from the next.
Among the pretty girls
my daughter is dancing, too.

michiyo nakamoto

SUMMER

(X)
In summer I wear panties
tinted lightly
like faded petals

A wet swimsuit
limp
at my feet

Every time I wear panties
    the summer creeps up

My face
reflected
in the faded mirror of the dressing room

My body
cooled in the sea
but still cold

A long way
I still don't know
where to return to.

(Y)
Flower, flowers aimlessly
into the night

Day after day
I plant them and they blossom
each second filling up
and collapsing

Our short summer
shorter nights
under the blurred half moon
in the presence of a distant evil

Still, it has nothing to do with them
they live
only by their own numbers

Our summer
the water at the bottom of a bucket
sand in the water.

(Z)
The Lena Flows into the Arctic Ocean
my heavy overcoat
ice in the ocean scrapes the bottom of a ship

The captain has a bright glimmer in his eye
this is the summer.

From here on in the land stands tall
the doors of the dark, empty houses are all lined up
I almost fall, head over heels
my heavy leather shoes.

The captain goes back
to his wife and daughter,
this is the summer.

LIVING THING

a   a   a   a

a long string
a swaying string in the water
a group of long string in the water
a swaying long flat string strings in the water

long strings in the water

I hate it

a current under the water
a lake in a dream
a small boat at the edge

                                              I hate it

Still . . .

a dream left
in an empty house
in the abandoned village

alone

an eyelid
trembling.

ILLUSIONS

                              —to live a summer
                                is to live a life

        the day breaks on the grass
      spirits of the night dissolve in green
          some things that are people,
  and illusions walk beyond the grass

I wonder if the grave will be dug up?
I wonder if the flesh has already vanished?

If I should trace the summer path, I could go anywhere
if so—

I too am on the verge of vanishing at noon

flowers hide the deep fragrance
and grow to the empty sky
but blood is sprouting from its roots

I was bathed in the bloody spray
I was soaked to the skin
round flowers
flat flowers

in the distant sky, airplanes come and go
I feel only the roaring sound trembling
in that sky there are still many people

what is the use of blood?
the long and slender flowers

the exhaust fumes hang over
in the afternoon of the flowers
I smell of a desert burning
I walk endlessly and live only when walking

don't I?

that other me is an illusion
the real me is in the other side of eternity
in the bloody spray.

kiyoko ogawa

FOR YOUR EIGHTH BIRTHDAY

When you were born
Your father was away.

Now you are eight,
And he is abroad.

During those eight years
He came and went.

Again and again.
Though men may praise his diligence

You ask me to get you
Another, better father.

"Next time," I say.
But when you grow,

You grow.
And when you overcome solitude

You overcome
Yourself.

JAPAN

The slope is sick from motorcycle exhaust
And deafened by the noise.

An old woman is eating a late lunch inside
Outside, her flowerpots are old and cracked.

Trash bags spill over with garbage
Where schoolgirls in uniform walk.

Two dogs copulate in a petshop cage
The act being watched by a man, who sees me.

They sell thin tatami mats in the supermarket
Little tomatoes rot at the bottom of a plastic container.

A construction worker digs by the roadside
A pregnant woman with her infant walks by.

The railroad crossing flashes its warning light
Fluorescent orange and white

So that no one will die.

CONDOMINIUM

"Happy New Year? Are you well?
            Last November I gave birth to a baby boy.
                I'm very busy taking care of him."

                    This year, something went wrong
                and I am obliged to see
            New Year's cards* addressed to someone else;
    similar messages to similar people.

kyong mi park

CHIMA CHOGORI

I felt it swaying there
People came and went
In the dusty underpass in Shinjuku
While it swelled with air, breathing deeply.
For a short time I stood before
The woman who wore it, staring
Until she disappeared into the crowd.

A dark blue *chima chogori.**

Its white collar
Smoothed the nape of her neck
It breathed calmly at her breast
It was
Something that moved
Something free
Melting the painful core beneath.

Its familiar scent rose like an affectionate look.
It seemed to be a short time
It seemed to be a long time
I remember it clearly,
It had happened before.

It used to be that I'd get irritated
Whenever anyone said
"traditional Korean clothing"
Taking offense at the Japanese
Who said *chima chogori* were wonderful.
I was even too ashamed to walk with my grandmother
When she wore one.

But for a very long time
In that tunnel in Shinjuku,
The dark blue folds
Opened happily to the wind

And I knew that you were me
And would always be.

yufuko shima

FLEETING LOVE

the light of a feast   in the intermittent darkness
your back waits & then   stands still
urged on by the sound of the snakeskin *shamisen*
my *geta* are growing impatient

led by the hand that steps on gravel
where the shadow of the Takakura Granary lowers its voice
we go under
the adan tree's branches
on my back
toward the moon   you kiss me on the lips

the swaying waves   we gaze at
sitting by the sea
my dangling legs trembling
one *geta* disappears on the beach

your fingers running through the black hair
that hides my cheeks
fingers speaking in whispers
I will leave here tomorrow

days passing by the window
gathering lost composure
a child smiles
in the hopes of capturing
its mother's heart

that was so long ago   what has become of it now?
fingers halfway   resting on the lips
looking up at the sea   the moon recedes
this thing called fleeting love
comes back in pieces.

IN COUNT BASIE'S SOUND

In the middle of the day
it gives a feeling to my presence
bringing hope & despair & joy & sorrow
such breath lying at MIDNIGHT BLUE
since then I have not been able to sleep
since SPLANKY's tenderness

I've left myself
in the polished-up swell of sound

Who is that alto tickling me?
singing call-and-response with the drums
arguing with the brass
FANTAIL making the tails of the shaking sounds
fan out

They acted tough
but turned into shy
kind men
weaving a sound cradle, a hammock
in the shade of the trees
the wind slipping through
the piano   becoming sunlight
shining through the leaves of the trees
swaying with the leaves shadows on my eyelids
do I have to wake up?
or relaxed, can I sleep more deeply?
the *obligato*
of the mute trumpet murmurs
into my ears
Count Basie's Orchestra's eyes on me
I steal into LIL DARLIN'

This club
appearing in my sleep
greeted by the sound of applause
THE KID FROM RED BANK
a clear ball skims the keys
couples from the tables approaching
surrounding the piano player
who plays real good to me

No need for words
between Count Basie's Orchestra and the audience
The Harbour View Club is swingin'
with blooming smiles
how do you like this?
DUET's intro
joking behind his shoulders
drawing his jaws closer together
& swingin' the audience begins to move
the base nods to his fingertip with the usual pose
we don't mind leaving the soup cold
because for now we're satisfied
with this musical feast

AFTER SUPPER
adding another candle to the dying fire
with a sound

the old sympathetic bartender
listens to the drunken stories
his customers tell him.
That is the story
the sax with the sophisticated sound
often tells me.

FROM NEW YORK

An infra-red film   sticks to my eyes,
Both my feet are   stricken   by panic.
Both my hands are   autistic,
Cancerous cells are   beginning to   sprout
In my thoughts, but they   disappear.
And suddenly, my ears   suffer   from diabetes, unnoticed.

A shop window   in Halloween colors:
A witch who turns   into a shoe   and puts on a
        pumpkin—
Energetic autumn, whose leaves turn red   and yellow
And keep falling,   America
Ronald Reagan glaring from a   poster with   bloodshot eyes

In a city where men wash a historic-looking   church
        whole deracinés unfolding   their   respective life-size
        drama

with deep and rich   but at the   same time,
lonely and familiar   eyes
pass by   each other

Central Park, where bodies   are   found   every   year,
blows up the wind that came in   crawling on the
    ground
and turns the tinted leaves   in the woods
into butterflies in an   instant,
under which squirrels   run
in the silence of a bronze   statue
when night falls
loneliness   and loneliness   are tied to darkness,
and on a   square, bright
window pane, window pane, window pane
they create   a beautiful
almost sorrowful   human-like   joint
In   a   net pulled by the Muse's hand,
  becoming a grape in a cluster,
scooped up   from
Broadway to Greenwich Village
from 4 Patchin Place to 6 Patchin Place
from a room   where e.e. cummings once lived
   I look down over a   garden's neatly divided   small
    autumn

Marietty.   Mrs. Kessler.   Mrs. Snyder,
leaving me   yearning

toward   my mother
in the depths   of the three women's eyes.
"What has not turned out as I had hoped?"
inside of me   tired of   being confused
and   repeating   toward   tired of being tired

in the sky   where the moon is making clear footsteps
leaving the most of my heart
in New York   where I picked up the smell
    of a lemon that I almost forgot
I go to Rhode Island.

ryōko shindō

PUDDLE

blood and tears of the Ice Age
can even be found in the calyx of a rose.
I can't help feeling that
we're all just slowly vanishing
here in this diluvial age
when we're sleeping
with mammoths.

I can't help feeling that
the people I love are just piling up
in the ridges of the earth
holding up the sky
in no particular rush
to die
relaxed,
just reading,
and singing.

kazue shinkawa

EYES

eyes
catch the first sign of daybreak
catch "objects" and "shapes"
catch signals given and sent
and where I am now
faster and sharper than any other part of me

eyes
reveal the mist in the mirror
expose dreams, expose traps
the holes in the moon
the naked king
eyes glaring like switchblades

eyes
become wet with tears,
seeing the heart's open wound and all its pain

wet from "hello," wet from "goodbye"
from the death of the young unknown soldier
from the happy light of other people's homes
like two grapes in the rain

eyes
hold the evening's beautiful glow
hold roses, the horizon,
words of a letter sent by someone kind,
keeping these images
on the back of my eyelids
eyelashes at the edge.

HAIR

Some mornings I can't tie back my hair
like barley in someone else's field.
I didn't steal it, but I get scattered
and can't seem to do it well.

Sometimes at night my hair comes untied.
Climbing up a hill and creeping into a valley
like ivy covering a castle
it blocks my view.

Is it mine?
When I'm asleep
when I'm awake and get depressed
this obstinate grass continues to grow.

The place it grows is
certainly mine.
Yet it seems the one who planted it
can see it day and night
from a place I do not know.

EARS

I recall
gathering shells on the seashore
In my mother's womb.
Matching up two strange and rippled shells
I put them on each side of my face
and wore them like barrettes.

The murmur of the rising tide was the first to come in.
Pulled by the moon, waves gently foaming.
not knowing the shapes of things
I listened to the sounds the two shells caught:
The sound of a well bucket, the voice of a clock,

a horn honking from the street.
That's why I embraced the shapes of things
when I came into the world.

Yet,
"How lonely this girl's ears look!"
My mother said.
When I was older, my lover said so too.
My ears were unlucky.
But of course they'd look lonely
since I'd parted them to put them on.
The two shells would never, ever
have the chance to meet again.

BLOOD VESSEL

The darkness I hold is deep and vast,
even larger than all the nights
of a hundred million years together
where does it come from and where is it going?
there is a river, and an ancient dog straining to hear it.

On a day I hear my grandfather's cough
on a day I hear the cry of a baby yet to be born
my mother's stories and my mother's mother's stories
are told over and over again.

There are those who have disappeared into the mist
of the river above, singing children's songs
my older brother, my little sister,
many cousins from my childhood.

Flowing,
freezing in sorrow
foaming in joy
a fenced-in mill filtering continuously
never stopping
to take even the shortest rest.

SONG

The song that slips from the lips of a woman
after giving birth to her first child
is the sweetest song in the world.
It tames the wild mane of the distant raging sea
it makes the stars blink
it makes wanderers look back on their journeys
it lights red lamps from the branches of spindly apple trees
in desolate valleys even the wind has forgotten.
Oh, if not so,
how does a baby grow?
This fragile, unprotected being
if not so?

OTHER SIDE RIVER

ATCHI NO KISHI

ōku no toshiheta shishatachi no reikon oshiwakete
boku atchi no kishi ni wattate iku
shishatachi no mori   katsute no seijatachi no horobite
iki tsuku tokoro ni
kono boku mada ichido mo tanjō sura shita koto nai
boku iku no da

shikyū no akatsuki ni boku konton to chi no kaorikagi
niku no futon ni idakarenagara hotondo
umi no soko no mada mezamenai taiyō ni natte
nemutte ita
ōto to memai no nami no oshiyoseru naka
iku hyaku-man nenrai no tenchisōzō no setsuna o
amiibaa kara kyōryū jidai ni sashi kakaru bōfūu
no kisetsu ni hon no hito nigiri hodo no niku no yoroi no
naka de furuenagara
boku wa kaimen no yō ni taiban ni shigami tsuki
taete kita no da
mada kotai ni sura narani mae wa ekijō no ginga ni
natte hikui shikyū no dōmu o fuan ni moenagara
hikōshita
mata konton kara katachi ni nari hajimeru
atsui doro no kisetsu dewa
me mo hana mo naku kuchi mo nōzui mo nai node
boku wa zenshin o souru no sukoppu nishite
ōto shinagara chi no ō ni nukazuita no da
boku

あっちの岸

多くの年へた死者たちの霊魂をおしわけて
ぼく　あっちの岸にわたっていく
死者たちの森　かつての生者たちの亡びて
いきつくところに
このぼく　まだ一度も誕生すらしたことない
ぼく　いくのだ

子宮のアカツキにぼく　混純と血の香りかぎ
肉のフトンに抱かれながら　ほとんど
海の底の　まだ　めざめない太陽になって
ねむっていた
嘔吐とめまいの波の押し寄せる中
幾百万年来の天地創造の刹那を
アミーバーから恐竜時代にさしかかる暴風雨
の季節に　ほんの一握りほどの肉のよろいの
中で　ふるえながら
ぼくは海綿のように胎盤にしがみつき
たえてきたのだ
まだ　固体にすらならない前は液状の銀河に
なって　低い子宮のドームを不安にもえながら
飛行した
また　混純から　かたちになりはじめる
熱い泥の季節では
目も鼻もなく口も脳髄もないので
ぼくは全身をソウルのスコップにして
嘔吐しながら血の王にぬかづいたのだ
ぼく

ima motte me mo hana mo kuchi mo nai ga sudeni
amiibaa demo sakana demo naku
mirai no hito ni nari hajimete iru

ima hodo boku
chichi kara tōku (nan oku kōnen kurai kana?)
mata chichi ni chikai toki wa nai

mada hito ni naranai boku wa
haha no shikyū no yado de konton to seimei o tsukuru sagyō o shite
iru no da
kono haha desae yoku shiranai yawaraka na
chi no dōmu no uchigawa wa
soto no sekai yori akaruku shio no michita uchū da
ima
shikyū no sotogawa dewa hikishio ga hajimari sono naka o
chichi ga shi no kusari o hikizuri toki no nagare ni noserarete
sanma no yō ni oyoide iku no ga mieru
na mo nai kaisō no tsuma no
kaguwashii kami o aibushinagara

dakara koso yoru no yami no fukami no naka de
chichi wa aru kedo mienaime de
aru kedo fure e nai haha no kokoro ni
tesaguri de niziri yotte iku no da

tsuki akari no sabaku de
nihon no saboten ga togedarake no karada de
kaze ni furuenagara fureenai ai ni tsuite
shabette itari
mata

いまもって目も鼻も口もないが　すでに
アミーバーでも　魚でもなく
未来の人になりはじめている

今ほど　ぼく
父から遠く　（何億光年くらいかな？）
また父に　近い時はない

まだ人にならないぼくは
母の子宮の宿で　混純と生命を創る作業をして
いるのだ
この母でさえよく知らない　やわらかな
血のドームの内側は
外の世界より明るく　潮の満ちた宇宙だ
いま
子宮の外側では引潮がはじまり　その中を
父が死の鎖をひきずり　時の流れにのせられて
サンマのように泳いでいくのがみえる
名もない海草の妻の
かぐわしい髪を愛撫しながら

だからこそ　夜の闇の深みの中で
父はあるけどみえない目で
あるけど　ふれえない母の心に
手さぐりで　にじりよっていくのだ

月あかりの砂漠で
２本のサボテンがトゲだらけの体で
風にふるえながら　ふれえない愛について
しゃべっていたり
また

nihiki no umigame ga oki ni mukatte hijō ni yukkuri to
kurai chinmoku o tabenagara tsure datte
oyoide iku

sore wa hotondo zetsubōteki na ketsui ni nurete
atsuku dorodoro ni hikatte iru chichi to hahatachi da

da ga karera ga shi e no takusan no nengetsu o
korekara heru mae ni
karera no ishiki no soto mata muishiki no tanima o yogiri
boku mada
tanjō sura shita koto nai boku
shikyū no semai nodo yori ikinari shi ni
gesuikan o nagareru osui no yō ni
eien ni nazukerareru koto naku
tsumi o okasu koto sura naku
hikari to kūki no amasa o shirazu
iku no da

ikinari atchi no kishi ni
toshiheta shishatachi no reikon no mori e to
kono boku iku no da

２匹の海亀が沖にむかって非常にゆっくりと
暗い沈黙をたべながら連れだって
泳いでいく

それは　ほとんど絶望的な決意に濡れて
熱くどろどろに光っている　父と母たちだ

だが　彼らが死への沢山の年月を
これからへる前に
彼らの意識の外　また無意識の谷間をよぎり
ぼく　まだ
誕生すらしたことない　ぼく
子宮のせまいノドより　いきなり死に
下水管を流れる汚水のように
永遠に名づけられることなく
罪をおかすことすらなく
光と空気の甘さを知らず
いくのだ

いきなり　あっちの岸に
年へた死者たちの霊魂の森へと
このぼく　いくのだ

kazuko shiraishi

BIRD

bye bye blackbird
it's not hundreds of birds   nor thousands of birds
but what is always flying away is a single bird
bearing my ugly entrails
bird
each time I conceive you I lose my sight
in my blindness   I live by smelling the world
then all I have been before   dies
and a new blind life begins to blossom.

bye bye blackbird   on the stage
he sings   transformed into a bird
the audience turns into ten thousand ears   listening
then they're millions of wings
blinded they flap their wings   each becoming a bird-spirit
following the voice of the bird on stage
dancing over the dark seats

but who can tell the real bird
from the apparition? besides
bye bye blackbird
what is really taking flight from here?
the one who sings   doesn't know either   he's only
caught up in ecstasy and feeling
     now that something is flying away
the real thing may be his easy rhthym
     or it may be the softest loin of his soul
it might be the memory of the uneasy sinful star
or the lukewarm blood
splashing from the tulip-shaped brain of his child
sitting in the very first row.

Bye bye blackbird
I am a bird
whether I deny it
or accept me as I am
as long as this pointed beak that never stops pecking
and the wings in the habit of flapping
can't be torn from me
I am a bird today
I become a prayer
piercing skyward several times daily
only to be thrown back down to the ground again
or I am the entrails the falling bird bears
these huge, fallen birds gathered inside me

small birds   thin, precocious birds
even haughty and tender birds
some half-alive, groaning inside me
I bury these birds like an everyday habit
while other birds strip the skin from their bones
like an everyday habit I warm the eggs of future birds
so tenderly and desperately
they too will grow into grotesque birds
who'll rip the future apart with their beaks.

Bye bye blackbird
I've become that grotesque bird
and want to make that bird fly away   once and for all
I must make that bird fly away as strongly as it spouts
its blood
while I sing
my heart out.

MALE OR MONKEY STORY

Do you have any idea
      what I have kept
for a long time?
      a bitch
crawling around on my bed.

I'm completely absorbed
in preventing
   each flea from escaping her
body
   if I could be showered in
insults
   even if I didn't become a
female that holds a highly esteemed love
   in her pouch
like a kangaroo
   I wouldn't sniffle or cry
but every pouch has already
   belonged to a female
and I'm a long-armed monkey
   carrying a barren male
without a female   or a pouch.

Shake, shake, this is a shake—
Everyone twists their bodies
   in the monkey dance
everyone is in pursuit of a
   monkey after philosophy
otherwise, how could we go on living?

That woman loved me too much,
   my ex-lover, who is beyond my control
   noble and poor

besides, she's a poet and is beyond my control
every night I wait
    while that woman drowns herself in alcohol and semen
unable to resurface   I hate being loved by the hermit-witch
like divine filth.

Let me tell you about men—
    As for men, women know nothing about them
but confuse the blackboard   with the powerful chalk of love
every man (as I wish it) is a naked horse
    running at full speed on the prairie
into the richest future   his tail sticking up like a broom
forgetting the barren male
    typing his exalted numbers
unable to figure out clearly
    if his rocket will be launched into
another universe stuffing up the male.

Bye Bye female—
    This is an outdated song
women are bored and once again yawning
    since men sprinkled water on people's consciousness
the male's been pushing on passionately
    toward elimination.

That's why I'm utterly   defeated
what shall I do with this

flea I've caught?
I wonder: should I take this loving one
    back to the bitch on my bed
though the bloody universe shines vividly
    over the whole body of the flea,
like a glowing sunset
    the sky where every female begins
in the mild climate and chaos of a womb's daybreak
    the vagina's crimson canopy.

I'll go back
    to the place where I've kept nothing
to bed
    the bed is white
a woman without a tail   she sleeps there
    or is she   awake?
Yet the bed is always made   for one
    since I am a long-armed monkey
my hands stretch out in all directions
    fumbling in the darkness
like a blind masseuse
    sweetly and constantly in pursuit
then I am also a spider
    who eats its own head
and vomits out of its ass
    slowly groping, I am a
stretching spider-monkey

it is then that
I hold female inside male
        and in both sexes
I begin to live for the very
        first time.

OTHER SIDE RIVER

Through many old souls of the dead
I push my way over to the other side river
The forest the once-living died and reached
I, this being who has never been born
Make my way.

At the womb's *dawn*   I, smelling of chaos and blood
Wrapped in a pillow of flesh, almost transformed
Into the still-sleeping sun at the depths of the sea
Sleep
In the surging waves of nausea and giddiness
For millions of years   since the moment of Creation
As an amoeba
Through the season of floods
Up to the time of the dinosaurs
In an armor of a simple handful of flesh
I trembled, clinging to the placenta like a sponge

And I endured
Before I had a body
I was the liquid galaxy
Flying anxiously in the womb's low arc
Taking shape from the chaos again
In a hot muddy season
Without eyes, mouth or brain
My body was a shovel of the soul
Kneeling before the King of Blood, vomiting
I, still
Lacking eyes, nose or mouth
Neither amoeba nor fish
Become a man of the future.

Now or never, I
Am far away from my father (how many billions of light
    years?)
And yet close to my father at the same time
I, who have not yet become a man
In the womb's chamber, create
Chaos and a life
Inside a soft, bloody womb that even this mother
Does not know
Brighter than the outside world, a universe
Flown by the tide
Now
Outside the womb, the tide begins to ebb   in it

I see my father dragging the chains of death,
Carried on the passage of time
Swimming upstream like a fish
Caressing the sweetest hair
Of the wife of an unnamed seaweed.

That's why   in the depths of the night's darkness
My father walks with invisible eyes
Groping and edging up
To the untouchable mother's heart.

In a desert in the moonlight
Two cacti, their bodies full of thorns
Tremble in the wind, talking of
An untouchable love
Or two sea turtles
Swimming out to sea very slowly
Eating the dark silence
Together.

They are my father and mother, wet with an almost
      desperate Determination
Shining hot and muddy.

Before they inch towards their inevitable deaths over the
      years
I, passing outside their consciousness
In the valley of the unconsciousness

I, who have never been born before
Going through the womb's narrow throat to sudden death
Like dirty water running from a sewer
Forever unnamed
Having committed no crime
Not knowing even the sweetness of light and air
I will go

Suddenly   to the other side river
To a forest of old souls
I   this being   will go

harumi makino smith

SPIRIT CATCHER/LEO SMITH

As if digging the truth out from
Six thousand years of recorded history
Rhythm resonates between heaven and earth.
Before the creator's hand comes down
We must go to the top of that mountain.
Even though the past is painted by blood
Even though the future that we have to dream, now
Sounds like the tiny flutter of the *kotankor-kamui**
Who wakes up in the darkness to feel the righteous breath
Of human beings—
This is the gift of the natural mystic.

LET MY CHILDREN HEAR
MUSIC/CHARLES MINGUS

My life must have started from zero,
But was always followed by minus.
At the breakfast table, yes.
In the noises of town, yes.
In my mother's voice which called to me in the evening, yes.
The track that I have to step on
Was always a track to minus.
Let me say a soul is innocent
I haven't found the light to shine on the track to reach the
    plus
It's just that . . .
So minus-women, minus-men, and minus-children,
I absolve you—
Come here and listen to this music, and
Please love your own soul.

ATTICA BLUES/ARCHIE SHEPP

Chained in the bottomless marshpond
I dye my body as black as possible
Tomorrow I'll be blacker than today.

The days stand on unreasonableness
Historical questions crushed under their feet.

But I don't stop protesting
Even though I can't move when I'm held down
Even if my last blessing was the sound of my twisted neck,
I'd make you listen from underground.

IT'S AFTER THE END OF THE WORLD / SUN RA AND HIS INTERGALACTIC RESEARCH ARKESTRA

Eternity
The future that starts from today is everlasting time
Marching on
Life goes into the future
Death goes back to the past
Sensibility knows no bounds when traveling
Cosmic love is endless
Provided to each of us
If you say the earth is jail, you're a prisoner
If you say it's home, you're a child
But it's just
What's on your mind

The planet accepts you without saying anything
And gives you food for living.
Well, eat it
And get on my spaceship.

fumiko tachibana

WAY TO THE MOON

I rowed a boat to climb up the sun
out of place out of pace
you were shining in the night sea

I had long forgotten
I was the moon
and the moon was me

In the dark you saw
one side of my body
that was your own shadow

Who knew
I had long forgotten
I could wax

Who knew
I could even wane
and wash upon the shore

If you see shrubs and leaves turning color
if you hear wind and grass rustling in the dark voice
of the sea

You'll see my unborn hands
rowing a boat
to where I was meant to be.

DON'T BIND ME

(for Joseph LaPenta)

You're looking out the window
for more substance behind
the green apparition reflected on the glass
listening to music coming from the stage
played by people from the continent.

You whisper to me
"Everything in Japan came from the outside
no *shamisen* no *shakuhachi* no *koto*
nothing *is* Japan, you see."

I know you're trying to stop me
(don't stop me)
I know you're trying to teach me
(don't teach me)
I know you're trying to persuade me
(don't do anything for me, please).

You know, an incredibly long sash
has tortured me all these years
binding layers of me
around my freedom
to breathe.

Our misery—this island
of no choice
(don't push me or I'll drown)
this land of no choice
(don't push me
into Saturday night trains
full of people people people
coming from karaoke bars
alcohol on their breath).

Remember when you first came to Japan
with your dream of playing *shakuhachi*?
Now I hear music coming from myself
I am coming out of the old me
I am ready to move on.

THIS FEBRUARY SIDEWALK

I want to meander into your soul.
I've stayed here
in my old clothes
for too long
in a house
of windowless wall unspoken word and private jail.
You come to my
door, call out my name
I want to be more
than the mandarin
tree, I want to be
the fruit you pick
every day of our spring
the air bright around me
my heartbeat strong.

Now I'm out
but grown into this February sidewalk
the moon a sliver of glass
and you sitting there
crumpled and brittle as a leaf on the frayed edge
of a worn plastic bench
writing everything,
a dark white
in a corner
of this triangle park
the morning has blown cold and real.

BRAVER AT NIGHT
(after W. S. Merwin)

In the legless black air
I look around and see
moondrops looking around

not yet not yet
pale moonlight
stay with this old confusion

lying in my own self for so long
I remember a voice
whispering about a man in a wheelchair

the man lost his legs a moon ago
yet still claims
pain all around his toes

the wind blows outside the window
edging the frayed borders of light
and shadow on the earth

this body of mine is not what I possess
here I am a shadow the way you are
when we're in the same room

the pain revives, climbing on me
while I watch
the air turn to gray

the dawn is haunting—
if I jump out this window
am I even braver?

DIFFERENT STATIONS

When I was
on the mainland
I could hardly think
of anything important.
You were sitting quietly on a low tree branch
writing a letter
to someone far away.
Don't fall.
This branch of yours is old
and brittle
and there's nothing
but the swift cold flow if you fall.
Please oh please
no more words unfolded
no more heavy rocks dropped
in our garden.

Between you and me
there are many lines running, parallel railways.
I wonder why you've kept me
when you've taken a train
to another station.

chimako tada

SUMMER GRAMMAR

assertive summer
casually tilts its head and finds no words
(somewhere the sound of water
a memory recalled by the bitterness of bluebells!)
a snake in the shape of a question mark recedes into a bush

a disc of glaring light weighing down his back
a boy's open wound spitting salt
twilight drops a vast patch over the eye
(gently, you remove the plaster cast from the joint of a
    dream)

soon the stars will hold their ranks
until then, only the light of water
the ripples of eyes,
a soul will remain your delusions

boy with the fragile eyelashes
open your palm to the void
capture the last punctuation
(it will flash like a firefly's light
and escape down the distant river . . .)

DAYFLOWER*

one summer morning I walked on a path between rice
        paddies
and trembled at the thousand dewdrops there
though the night brought not a single drop of dew
to men's hearts.

how extravagant this slender leaf is
more brilliant than the tears of wily Caliban
I wonder, will we no longer offer foxtails and daisies
to the breeze in distant hair?

like a little girl everyone has scolded
crouched on the path, plucking petals from the dayflower
I can only dye my fingers sky blue.

PROLOGUE TO THE ADVENT

An ephemeral being is pregnant with an eternal man
The eternal man is amorphous,
Impossible to tell if it is man, woman, or monster

Snowflakes fall when the ephemeral being scratches her head
Oh, winter has come already
It is the season an annual Mary gives birth
To an annual Jesus

Like a bagworm hanging down from a window
The eternal man sways in dark amniotic fluid
A ripe persimmon, the setting sun quivers
Then drops.

*

Pithecanthropus head-over-heels arching your back
Before long you will be born an eternal man
Soon you will eat up eternity
And end up a mere *homo sapiens*

Leaves fall, revealing spiked branches
My slender neck is buried in a muffler of decaying leaves
I will drink warm sake to pierce my insides,
So that you will be drunk before you awake

I will raise a flesh-colored sail
Setting off by the ears of the wind
You can hang by the cord of the world's navel
And be carried by the wind from the sea

The curtain will soon rise
On the passion play of the Advent
The tiny eternal man transforms his hands and feet
Into drumsticks that beat the drum ardently from the inside

*

Each day you draw a map on the skin as dry as parchment
Walking relentlessly on a stiffened lifeline
At last, you slip from the palm of God

A gourmet that sucks the monkey's brain
Worm-eaten leaves on your windowpane
These are the calling cards of a frozen heaven

You, in the heated room,
Eating summer tomatoes after season's end
Leave the dinner table behind
And fill the sprinkler with fresh water.
A child is sprouting in the garden of God.

YESTERDAY'S SNAKE

I saw a beautiful snake in my dream yesterday.

Actually, it was not really a dream, but it was in my garden, surely, that I saw the snake. In a light rain, in the depths of the evening garden under the sheer rock whose surface alone was still left white.

But today, when the weather is good, the wet twilight snake does not appear.

Its body veiled in perfect scales, the large white and gray striped snake endured my gaze with a cool detachment, not even stirring.

(Behind me, the sound of a deep mountain stream rushed up.)

I blew a whistle to the earth where darkness was descending. The snake's tongue jutted out at once. Rather, his tongue jutted out and in again so quickly that I hardly saw it.

The pointed tremolo in pale vermillion . . .

Pulling his tongue in he began to move, terribly slowly, though the scales of his body trembled a dozen times each second as his body slid forward, quivering and smooth.

Three crests of a wave from head to tail, always the same, pushing his head out further and further, the tail disappearing.

(I wonder if people call this swift flashing life progress?)

The snake slid into thick grass near the roots of a pine tree, leaving me alone in the rain with an umbrella in my hand, like a tall mushroom, swaying, tilting.

Yes, surely that was a dream. A long and narrow dream that waxed and waned while wavering.

(That splendid white and gray *vibrato* of the scales covering its whole body!)

This garden, too, is not what it was yesterday. Dryness covers it. It has no shadows. Still, the sound of the mountain has become hollow.

Surely I must have kept my eyes wide open in the dark, illusory rain.

And I myself must have been a single mushroom in the corner of that garden.

SUMMER GRAMMAR

NATSU NO BUNPŌ

dangen no natsu ga
futo kubi o kashige zekku suru
(doko ka de mizu no oto
kikyō no nigami ni yomigaeru kioku!)
hebi wa gimonfu no katachi shite yabu ni modoru

gyakkō no enban o hikuku seotte
shōnen no kizuguchi wa mada shio o fuite iru
tarete kuru tasogare sōdai na gantai
(yume no kansetsu kara kimi wa sotto gipusu o hazusu)

yagate hoshitachi wa ikai ni tsuku darō

sore made wa mizu akari
me no sazanami
tamashii dake ga kimi no mayoi da

ore yasui matsuge o motsu shōnen yo
te no hira o kokū ni hirogete
saigo no kutōten o torae yo
(sore wa hotaru no yō ni tenmetsu shi
tōi kawashimo e nogaresatte shimau . . .)

夏の文法

断言の夏が
ふと首をかしげ　絶句する
（どこかで水の音
桔梗の苦みによみがえる記憶！）
蛇は疑問符のかたちして薮にもどる

逆光の円盤を低く背負って
少年の傷口はまだ塩をふいている
垂れてくるたそがれ　茫大な眼帯
（夢の関節からきみはそっとギプスをはずす）

やがて星たちは位階に就くだろう

それまでは水明り
眼のさざなみ
魂だけがきみの迷いだ

折れやすい睫毛をもつ少年よ
掌を虚空にひろげて
最後の句読点をとらえよ
（それは蛍のように点滅し
遠い川下へ逃れ去ってしまう……）

junko takahashi

IN A FIELD OF CLOVER

In a field of clover
I don't mind being blown about by the wind
    if it makes me happy
when the sky becomes a bright glowing red
I don't mind drinking sake
    if it makes me happy
I don't mind having five lovers
    if it makes me happy
I don't mind being reborn as a cat
    if it makes me happy
I don't mind turning over a new leaf
    if it makes
    me
    happy.

IN SUMMER

On the train
the woman in front of me
read a passage with the caption
    creating the Buddha but forgetting the soul
but when I glanced at it again
it said
    creating the Buddha but not forgetting the soul
it seemed like a how-to manual
and not a religious book at all.

Crossing the bridge
the train's roar
mingled with the cry of locusts.
the river sparkled in the sun
and I wondered:

How to?
How to live?

GLOVES

I tended a plant in my room and now it's growing
Wonderful to have something growing by my side

when one side outgrows the other, I turn the pot around
my plant seems confused at first, but then calms down
the spring sun shines on my notebook
the grass which is me lets the spring warmth
reach down to its cells
and heads off to work

the tips of the grass have not yet formed a hand
but since I don't get home from work 'til late
I keep gloves
in my pocket
just the same.

THE BIG SEA

Rocks were made from tetrapods
the sands have risen within the year
or should I say the sea has fallen?

My original view was a stretch of water unhindered by rocks
it is the Pacific Ocean I can't be sure of
unless I look around.

I gather seashells on the shoaling beach
discovering newborn shellfish

soon the waves will nurture the shells
before they swallow them.

Waves scrape the sides of the tetrapods
making them pebbles and then swallowing them.
The big sea will come back once more
within a me who will no longer exist.

taeko tomioka

STILL LIFE

Your tale has ended
By the way, what did you have for a snack today?
Your mother said yesterday
I want to die soon.
You took your mother's hand
And wandered nowhere in particular
You were gazing at a sand-colored river
You were gazing at a landscape with river
One day one of Bonnard's women said
In France they call a willow "tree of tears"
You said yesterday
Mother, when did you give birth to me?
Your mother said
I didn't give birth to a living thing.

THE STORY OF MY LIFE

Because dad and mom
and the midwife
and bookies all over
bet on a boy,
I just had to
tear out of the placenta as a girl.

Then
since everyone praised me
I become a boy.
Then
since everyone praised me
I become a girl.
Then
since everyone was mean to me
I dared to become a boy.

When I came of age
my sweetheart was a boy
so there was nothing to do but become a girl.
Then
since everyone except my sweetheart
said that I'd become a girl
I went back to being a boy.
Too bad because my sweetheart

said he wouldn't sleep with me
if I were a boy
so I became a girl again.

Before long, several centuries passed.
Now the poor started a bloody revolution
ruled by a piece of bread
so I became a medieval church
saying *for love, for love*
as I wandered the alleys
passing out old clothes and riceballs.

Several more centuries passed
this time God's Kingdom had come
and rich and poor lived as one
I scattered propaganda from my helicopter.

Before long, several more centuries passed
this time
bloody revolutionaries
knelt down before the rusty cross
and saw the fire of order in disorder.
There in a basement tavern
I played cards and drank
with Byron, Musset, Villon, and Baudelaire
Hemingway and the girls in black pants
we debated
what it meant to be a libertine
in that country in the Orient called Japan

making fun of things like
the simultaneity of love.

Because dad and mom
and the midwife
and everyone else
said I was a child prodigy
I became a philistine
they said I was a fool
so I became an intellectual
and built a house out back
not knowing what to do
with all of my excess energy.

Once my reputation
as an intellectual out back had grown
I went out front
and started to walk.
My walk was that of my dad and mom
And I, their changeling
was at cross-purposes
agonizing over
the changeling's honor.
So I became a boy
for my sweetheart
who by then had become a respectable girl,
and made him stop complaining.

WILL YOU MARRY ME?

I never go anywhere—
I've cut down all the trees in my backyard
and pulled up all the grass around me.
People bore children
and the children went to war
when they came back
the children bore children—
there are children everywhere.
But the women, they simply bathe.
It will all be over soon
perhaps the grass will grow
and people will die in the grass.

mieko watanabe

VILLAGE

all roads lead to that village
the small village where a cold wind blows from the moun-
    tains
in the afternoon

the villagers all had red eyes
but yours were green like mine.
And you were deaf and dumb
all of them were insane
that's what you told me

oppressed by our green eyes
we had to live at the far end of the village
growing vegetables and flowers

one night three years ago
they set our house on fire

you threw a cat into a well
and ran away into the mountains laughing
your eyes turning cold gray

there's a girl who looks like you
she lives in the village now
her eyes are red
she speaks their language fluently.

YOU, THE DESERT WIND

Disappear,
everything that I love
drying
forever drying
each drop of blood flowing out
what kind of life
what kind of promise
can I call this
river flowing steadily?

You,
the desert wind
in the far-away west
at the crossroads of fire

falling
blood disappearing
world ending.

Burn,
my madness
my now
at the heart of this crossroads
the bridges people build
over one another.

michiko yamamoto

THE RED HAT I WON'T LET LOOK UP AT THE SKY

I've never heard the voice of beautiful words. Whenever word order is connected to a voice, to me it's like each word is tearing down the stones of a thick wall. The sound is very intense, loud and painful for me, so whenever I want to hear beautiful words I take a small red straw hat out of its box and put it on my head.

I walk along a crowded street. I stop at a manhole. I come to a bridge. Leaning over the rail, I look at the muddy water below.

I stop into the confectionery shop. I buy Baumkuchen. I buy Mont-blanc. I buy giraffe-shaped chocolates. I buy milk chewing gum.

I stop into the fruit-seller. I buy a lemon. I buy a bunch of grapes. I buy lots of strawberries. I buy some walnuts. I buy pomegranates.

I stop into the flower shop. I buy a yellow lubinus. I buy

yellow roses. I buy a royal purple hyacinth. I buy a Buckingham chrysanthemum.

I stop into the toy shop. I buy a baby turtle. I buy large boots. I buy a small baby carriage. I buy fireworks. I buy magic secrets. I buy a pistol for my sweetheart.

I stop into the variety store. I buy an ashtray woven from grass. I buy an ugly duckling.

I buy an old, cold thermometer once used by the moon.

I buy a bone plucked from a jellyfish.

I buy a magic stick and a witch's silk shoes.

The red hat gets wet in the rain that has just begun falling. I wait for the bus in front of the Komatsu store. When it stops raining, the evening takes on a slight chill. The sky over the village is a tangle of purple and orange and gray. Two poets pass by on the damp, darkened asphalt. They walk on, deep in conversation. The bus comes.

I want to hear beautiful words. Sitting in the bus on the swaying seat, I take the red hat off. Words drop from the hat, scattering surreptitiously. The passengers are transformed into words. They become quiet, like words. The silent words sway.

I have just bought quite a lot of words.

The small red hat should not look up at the sky. When it looks up from my head, the words fly into the sky, and riding the bus becomes boring once again.

WALKING BONE, RUNNING FLESH

Since the forest took root in the palm of the hand
like lines with a touch of intricacy
The Way went running away, branching off meaningfully,
stretching, becoming crooked, and winding.

It was the starting point of a logical connection
which looked like the evening scenery stretching in deep
    black
carrying fragile whim like a line from the heart
where the slender bare white feet of a dwarf
were seen to surge on.
In the cave where no one can tell
morning from night or day
the logical connection gave the walking bone
the chance to wander countries,
and the running flesh a molecule of thought.

A woodkeeper—(who must have something like a personal
    motivation
for there is no guidepost at all),
it's hard to believe that electric current
becomes remote from the sky
and the logical connection that is like a line from the heart
while explaining, in illusions, that there is a bench at the
    terminal point—

showed me the pure white bare feet of the dwarf
only the feet walking further ahead in dim white,
    surging on.

On its way, the bone lay down
in a strange second-rate facility
and tested its appetite carefully.
The flesh, however, told its companion
it's a shame to lose a day's schedule
and left, staring at the running, running bare feet
    of the dwarf's short steps.
. . . what the bone discovered after the flesh hurried down
was a brand-new way which gave off a fate-like smell
and put up a name plate without permission.
"A fatal way, this is,"
the bone walked away, rattling as he went.
Breaking away from the senses.

The bone
on the way named Fate
walked away, resting in a corner
so as to move like a machine.
The deep wood took the roots on the palm of man's hand
and at the same time, the reason why
the flesh and the bone—who started together—
broke the pledge on their way,
was a difference of suspicious opinions on earth.

Persistently, the flesh
(deciding not to have a good appetite)
ran without rest, aided by two feet.
A deep rotten body of water, clammy and polished in oil
identified as a lake and a marsh even from a distance,
it looks like an evening scene
went over on two feet fearlessly and tempted the flesh,
causing it to suffer and making it troubled
but pretending to ignore all these things earnestly
jumped over a stump that looked like a beast,
turned around and winked at the flesh.

The flesh lived in comfortable hardship
and kept on running to catch up with those two white
     small feet.
The bone walked awkwardly without a goal
driven by the illusion of the dark night
Whither and for what am I going?
The thought sometimes occurred to him.

Certainly the bone walked in different ways, clumsily.
It took a rest and adopted itself to the regular star system
and sometimes became hot-blooded and urgent thinking
     of the flesh
so, contenting him slightly it walked away, rattling.

The forest that took its roots in the palm of the hand
was gradually beset with wrinkles
and as soon as it withered and leaves began to fall,
knowing that, like it or not,
they were held together by this manifest pledge
they knew they would have simply become scum
so the bone walked
and for its part, the flesh ran.

hiroko yoshida

DOOR

The door
I can never
seem to find
is the one
that I must open.
When I try
to get along without
asserting myself
the door hits against me
whether I like it
or not
breaking me
from bosom to back
forcing me
to know how I feel
gaining time
countless doors

my blood
I destroy
how long
must this last?
the voice of ears
softly murmur
each holding a difference
I myself can't grasp.
Losing my balance
I open the
door,
not knowing
which one
it is.

FLYING

Along the earth's axis
we fly towards a certain direction
under the same sky
we each do our own thing

If I get you into a corner
a handful of sky carrying me
will be engulfed by the earth's shadow

will you be beyond my reach
intangible
the small gap between us
a manifestation of our love
let's draw the line without saying a word.

Last night
I parted from the flock
and turned around toward the man who followed me
the man I cannot love
perhaps I
can only capture your sky
can only shout
I love you
as I fly off
by myself.

sachiko yoshihara

NONSENSE

The wind is blowing
The tree stands.

Yes, nights like these
You stand, the tree.

The wind is blowing
The tree stands, a sound is heard.

Alone, I play with bitter lather
in my bathtub late at night,

Breathing out the bubbles like a crab
In the lukewarm water.

A slug is crawling
On the wet tiles

Yes, late nights like these
You crawl, the slug.

I sprinkle salt on you
You disappear and yet remain.

What fear is: existing
Or not existing.

Once again, spring has come
Once again, the wind is blowing

I am a salted slug
I don't exist, not anywhere.

Surely the lather
has carried me away

Yes, nights like these
I'm carried, me.

SUNSET

Clouds set
Be with me

Birds burn
Be with me

The sea escapes
Be with me

Before long
All things become one

> *Fingers trace*
> *Time unscented*
> *Death stirs*

Ants sleep
Be with me

Winds stumble
Be with me

Before long
The dream is over

And silence
Covers all.

RESURRECTION

I kill love not to intend to die   this is self-protection
the pistol I pointed at you is aimed at my heart
with the heat of crime and the coldness of punishment
a crack runs inside of me   I should split apart   from there
a hole opens like an illusion   and extends to death
        perhaps calmly
the dripping soul of the world recedes   followed by
beside the window of   a long, long solitary cell   may be
death that is not quiet   burning death   burning life
in the rain   wet with its own sweat   the spider's
painting   out   narrowing   shining zero ellipse

tsuneko yoshikawa

IF YOU

i.

If you
    stay silent
        who will tell everyone
            about that day?

If you
    do not talk
        who will speak to everyone
            of that morning?

If you
    run away
        who will make everyone aware
            of that moment?

If you stay silent
No one will know your sister's and brother's final cries for
    water
Oh our houses our trees our lovers are burning!
Mother! My back is burning   the earth is burning

Yet, those who died
    Utter no words of resentment.

ii.

If the poets stay silent
    who will tell you
        of the flash and flame
            in that evil moment?

If the poets do not speak
    who will tell you
        of the demon skin that melted so unnaturally?

If the poets run away
    who will make the words known
        Epitaph*

"Forever carved in stone
A shadow thrown on the sand
Between between heaven and earth, fallen
The spirit of a flower"

iii.

If you stay silent

   No one will ever know of your suffering
Oh heaven and earth collapsing! buildings stones girders
   cities   children hearts the
earth   all

                          fallen

The great resentment of those slaughtered
    the rising spirits
        a million voices of revenge from those who died
            while running wailing groaning

Give back
   bring me back to life
      give me back my relatives
         give the people back*

            give back

If I   had been alive
I could not
have forgiven.

CITY OF STRANGERS
(in the voice of a dead girl)

6th of August, 1990
walking in the
city of   strangers
the overpass
the days of youth

     where am I? who are you?

beyond the gigantic columns of clouds
a spaceman's white hand stretches out
    becoming the mushroom cloud

              the overpass is gone, the meeting hall too

this is not an illusion
in the intense heat
the crisp, cold, clear   air

a funeral train passes through Chernobyl
Kichijōji, Ogikubo, and Koganei
full of wandering dead, relatives unknown
a child without arms
cows, deer with three legs
a procession from Hiroshima

marches through Chernobyl
duckweeds bloom
against the crimson sun
Paris and New York
don't want to be another Hiroshima
who will see
the last person on earth?

In August,
the eight-year-old girl who died
in Hiroshima
the sorrow, tears and danger of the bomb
will always be with us.

notes

Poems by the following poets were translated by Akemi Tomioka and Leza Lowitz: Saho Asada, Mieko Chikapp, Chuwol Chong, Misao Fujimoto, Hiromi Itō (except "Harakiri"), and Iro Kitadai. Poems by Yuri Kageyama, Kiyoko Ogawa, and Fumiko Tachibana appear here in their original English-language text. Keiko Matsui Gibson and Harumi Makino Smith translated their own poems. All translations for other poems in this volume (including "Harakiri" by Hiromi Itō) are by Miyuki Aoyama and Leza Lowitz. The following text notes are referenced by page number:

36   "Comfort women" was the name given to the thousands of Chinese, Korean, Southeast Asian, and some European women forcibly taken from villages, towns, and POW camps in the Japanese Empire and forced into sexual slavery at "sexual comfort facilities" near the front lines to "service" the Japanese Imperial Army during its invasion of China in the late 1930s. According to Ian Buruma in his book *The Wages of Guilt*, most of these comfort women died of disease, murder, or enemy fire, but those who survived were greatly ashamed of their dark history. In 1991, former comfort women from South Korea traveled to Japan to demand compensation from the Japanese government, a request which was ignored. When Kim Young Sam, the first democratically elected civilian president of South Korea, was asked what the Japanese government should do to compensate the former Korean

sex slaves of the Imperial Japanese Army, he spoke for all comfort women when he answered, "It is not your money we want. It is the truth we want you to make clear. Only then will the problem be solved."

38 *Yaishamena* refers to a love song. *Tekunpe* is a shield for the back of the hand. *Makiri* is a pocketknife.

49 Jizō is the patron saint and guardian of small children. Buddhists believe that the souls of dead children end up at Sai-no-kawara, a river separating them from Paradise. A witch waits by this river to steal the children's clothes. Jizō chases the witch away and hides the children in his robes. There are hundreds of stone Jizō statues along well-traveled roads in Japan. They are adorned with biblike collars in bright red colors that have been presented by the mothers of dead and aborted children to clothe the child-spirits whose clothing has been stolen by the witch.

50 *Kana* are the Japanese written characters that represent syllabic sounds.

52 *Fudo-myōō* is an avenging Buddhist deity.

69 In Sanskrit, *preta,* the name of the cats who lived in the Buddhist hell of starvation.

Ju Ri was the name given by men to Okinawan women sold into prostitution in the Ryukyu Islands, now a part of Japan that encompasses Okinawa and a chain of fifty-five islands in the Pacific between Japan and Taiwan. Derogatory *kanji* (Chinese characters) were used for the words describing the women. In the poem, the speaker "takes back" the words Ju Ri and writes them first in *kana* as "Ju Ri" and finally in *katakana* (the syllabary used for imported words) as "Bi Rui." The Okinawan language is written and pronounced differently from mainland Japanese, and "Bi Rui" would be "Ju Ri" in Okinawan dialect.

75 The Kamakura period (1185-1333) was the first feudal age in Japanese history.

86 Masaya Oki (born 1952) was a handsome and extremely popular

television and film actor who often portrayed macho men. He committed suicide in 1983 by jumping off Tokyo's Keio Plaza Hotel in downtown Shinjuku. Like Yukio Mishima, a well-known author who killed himself a decade earlier, Oki was bisexual. At the time of his death he left a suicide note to his lover. It read, "Father, I will wait for you in Nirvana."

On March 14, 1701, Asano Naganori, a nobleman, drew his sword in Edo Castle and attacked Kira Yoshinaka, one of the shogun's chief aides. Asano only succeeded in wounding the man, but the shogun promptly ordered him to commit *harakiri* to atone for his act. This he did, leaving his forty-seven retainers masterless samurai, or *rōnin*. Two years later, the now-famous Forty-Seven Rōnin broke into Kira's mansion to finish off the job. They were arrested and allowed to disembowel themselves collectively—as an honorable act of clemency. Forty-seven cherry trees were planted at their death spot in their memories, and they still bloom there to this day. The story of the masterless samurai is considered to epitomize Japanese notions of vengeance and loyalty, and it has been retold countless times in books, the theater, and film

90 A quotation from artist Joseph Beuys, whose performance at the René Block Gallery in New York in 1974 was an action piece in which he caged himself with a coyote to create a spiritual connection.

92 Chant from the Buddhist text *Hannya Shinkyō*: "We have reached the other bank of the River (Nirvana)."

104 *Tanzaku* are narrow white strips of paper on which haiku is written. *Saijiki* refers to a dictionary giving the appropriate seasons and other references for items appearing in haiku.

105 *"Umai—jitsuni umai"*: "Superb, definitely superb." Hanayagi is the largest school of Japanese classical dance. Japanese classical arts are run by families, with the eldest child inheriting the position of *iemoto*, the master teacher who is head of the household.

109   A reference to two clans of medieval Japan who made war on each other until the victory of one led to the creation of a new military government in Kamakura.

110   Ottakai is an island in the Woleai Group in Micronesia. The island was invaded by the Japanese Army in World War II.

111   A *dagoba* is a wooden board (stupa) placed by the grave of the dead. Buddhist blessings are written on the wood by a priest.

146   During New Year's in Japan, it is customary to send postcards, or *nengajō*, to one's business associates, friends, and acquaintances. The average person sends out over two hundred of these cards—and many send up to two thousand. Most people have their own printers to save time and stamp out the same message on each card.

147   A *chima chogori* is a long, flowing, traditional Korean skirt and blouse.

178   In the Ainu tradition, many living things are deified. In this belief, the *kotankor-kamui* is the Big Owl, the highest-ranking God.

190   "Dewflower" in Japanese.

224   These lines are from "Epitaph" by the poet Tamiki Hara, who was born in Hiroshima in 1906 and experienced the atomic bomb firsthand. He wrote about his experience in several novels and books of poetry. "Epitaph" was part of a series entitled "Time of Evil" and was published in January 1949. Hara committed suicide in 1951.

225   These are lines from Hiroshima poet Sankichi Tōge's collection of poetry *Give the People Back* (1950). Tōge was almost two miles from the epicenter of the atomic bomb when it fell on August 6, 1945. He survived injuries from the flying glass and metal, but died from radiation sickness in 1953 at the age of thirty-six. Tōge published a second volume of poetry, *Atomic Bomb Poems* (1951).

about the poets

For convenience and to give a better idea of the nature of the published material cited here, most Japanese-language titles of books and articles have been translated into English. For a list of books that have been published in English, see the Bibliography. Yuri Kageyama, Kiyoko Ogawa, and Fumiko Tachibana write in English.

Miyuki Aoyama teaches American literature at Seitoku University in Chiba Prefecture near Tokyo. She is a published poet and literary critic (including coeditor of this anthology), as well as the Japanese translator of H.D. and the poetry of Erica Jong. She lives in the Japanese countryside with her family. The mother of two children began writing nine-line poems during her first pregnancy.

Saho Asada is a lesbian mother and novelist, poet, and essayist. He has been published in two collections, *Just One Thing* (199? *Will Meet Eachother Somewhere in the World* (1994).

Mieko Chikapp, an Ainu, was born in 1948. She is an emb who works in her own as well as traditional Ainu desi learned from her mother as a child. She also perfo and writes poetry. She gave herself the name Chik "bird" in the Ainu language, to reflect her hope t freely as a bird within Japanese society. She ha world as a participant in aboriginal rights and tion conferences, and is actively involved ir Japanese homogeneity. Her work reflect renewal of Ainu culture. Chikapp has published *Blessings of the Wind: The Culture and Human Rights of the Ainu People* (1991) and *The Spirit of Ainu Design in Embroidery* (1994).

Chuwol Chong (Japanese name: Shūgetsu Sō) is a second-generation *zainichi* (Japanese resident of Korean nationality) who was born in Japan in 1944. She has published two books of poetry: *The Collected Poems of Shūgetsu Sō* (1970) and *Ikaino, Women, Love, Poems* (1984), and two books of poetry/essays, *Ikaino Performance* (1986) and *I Love You* (1987). The mother of three children, she lives in Osaka, where there is a strong *zainichi* community.

Misao Fujimoto is a *burakumin*. She was born into an extremely poor family and did not learn to read or write until her later years. Her poem in this book came out of her experience attending anti-illiteracy classes. Fujimoto now works as a cook in a nursery school.

Keiko Matsui Gibson received a Ph.D. in comparative literature from Indiana University in 1992 for her dissertation entitled "Noma Hiroshi's Struggle for the Total Novel: Critical Absorption of Balzac, Joyce, and Sartre." She has taught comparative literature at universities both in Japan and in the U.S., and has published translations, critical studies, poems, and essays in a variety of publications. Her book of poems, *Stir Up the Precipitable World!*, was published in 1983. She is married to the American poet Morgan Gibson.

Toshiko Hirata was born in 1955 and received her education at Ritsumeikan University. Her books of poetry include *Scallions Repaying Acts of Kindness, Restrained Atlantis*, and *A Woman Grows Fatter by Night*. She is one of a few women prose poets in Japan today.

Kiyoko Horiba was born in Hiroshima Prefecture in 1930. She studied Japanese literature at Waseda University and worked for the Kyōdō News wire service for nine years, beginning in 1954. Since 1982 she has published her own magazine of poetry and essays, entitled *Ishtar*. She has published several books of poems, including *Sky* (1962), *Old Man, Various Phases* (1974), and *Shuri* (1992), for which she received the Modern Poets Award in 1993. She has also written many volumes of essays, including *American Back Window* (1968), *Takamure Itsue* (1977), and *Seitō: Critical Essays on Women's Liberation* (1991). She is currently at work on a book about the American Occupation Army's censorship of writings on the atomic bomb.

Noriko Ibaragi was born in Osaka in 1926. She was a founding member of the influential postwar group poetry group Kai (Oar) with well-known poets Shuntarō Tanikawa and Makoto Ōoka. She addresses social and political themes in her work and has written eight volumes of poetry, three volumes of essays, and a volume of translations. Her best-known books are *Dialogue* (1955), *Requiem* (1965), and *A Small Present* (1982).

Yohko Isaka was born in Tokyo in 1949. She studied Japanese literature at Sophia University and worked as a high school teacher until 1985. Isaka is the author of nine volumes of poetry and has also published collected essays and volumes of literary criticism. Her major works are *A Morning Gathering* (1979), *GIGI* (1982), which received the "H" Award in Poetry, and *A Violin Family* (1987).

Rin Ishigaki was born in Tokyo in 1920. She worked full-time at a bank for forty-one years while raising a family and writing poetry. Her work addresses the struggles of working women in Japan. She has written numerous volumes of poetry and essays, including *The Pan, The Iron Pot and the Fire Burning Before Me* (1959), *Brief Outline of a Career* (1979), and *Tender Words* (1984).

Hiromi Itō was born in Tokyo in 1955 and studied at Aoyama Gakuin University in Tokyo. Itō is an unconventional poet with exceptional vigor, concerned with the physiological sensations of motherhood and the mysteries of the life and death cycle. Her works include the poetry books *The Plants and the Sky* (1987), *The Princess* (1979), *The Collected Poems of Hiromi Itō* (1980, 1988), *Green Plums* (1982), *On Territory 2* (1985), *On Territory 1* (1987), and *Family Art* (1992). She has also published three collections of essays: *Woman's Folklore* (1986), *Tummy, Cheek, Bottom* (1987), and *Good Breasts, Bad Breasts* (1985; subsequently made into a film). She currently lives in Kyushu.

Yuri Kageyama was born in 1953 in Aichi Prefecture and grew up in bilingual and bicultural households in Japan, Maryland, and the American South. Her first book of poems, *Peeling*, was published in 1988 by Ishmael Reed in California (I. Reed Books, Co.). Her works have appeared in various anthologies including *Breaking Silence: An Anthology of Contemporary Asian American Poets*, *Stories We Hold Secret: Tales of Women's Spiritual Development*, *Nikkei America*, *Canada Shishu*, and *Touching Fire: Erotic Writings by Women*. She has been published widely in America and in Japan. Educated at Cornell University and the University of California at Berkeley, she confesses a weakness for American jazz and Japanese fashion designer Yohji Yamamoto.

Ritsuko Kawabata was born in Hokkaido in 1919. She has taught primary school for almost fifty years. Her book of poems, *The Flower That Never Withers*, was published in 1983.

Iro Kitadai was born in 1904. She is a *burakumin* who was seventy years old before she learned to write her own name, and the poem in this anthology reflects her tremendous optimism and lack of bitterness toward Japanese society. Iro Kitadai died in 1983.

Masayo Koike has written two volumes of poetry, *Beginning at the Canal Town* (1988) and *Festival of Green Fruit* (1991). She received the *La Mer* Award in Poetry in 1989, and her poems have appeared in various literary magazines, including *Gendaishi Techō* and *La Mer*. She writes poetry to bring out the magic of the Japanese language and plans to write a book for children. She also plays the viola.

Rumiko Kōra was born in Tokyo in 1932 and received her education at Tokyo Metropolitan University of Fine Arts and Keio University. Her first collection of poetry, *Students and Binds*, was published in 1958, and her second collection, *Place*, in 1963. A poet and prose writer, Kōra was well known for her opposition to the Vietnam War and for her study of America's influence on Japanese politics and economics. She is particularly interested in the Afro-Asian literary movement and the Women's Liberation movement. In addition to her poetry, which has been inspired by the French Structuralists and

American Objectivist poets, she has published three volumes of essays, three books of feminist criticism, three translations of poetry, and two novels.

Teruko Kunimine was born in Takasaki in 1934. Her books of poems include *The Onion's Black Box* (1987), *4 x 4 = 16: Late Shopper on the Moon* (1989), and *Drifters* (1991). She is also a pianist and teacher of music composition.

Kiyoko Nagase was born in 1906 in Okayama Prefecture. She has written sixteen volumes of poetry, four volumes of prose poems, and many volumes of essays. Her main works are *Grendel's Mother* (1948), *To the One Who Comes at Daybreak* (which won the Earth Award and the Modern Women's Poetry Award), and *Himiko, Himiko*. Kiyoko Nagase died in February 1995.

Michiyo Nakamoto was born in Hiroshima Prefecture in 1949 and received her education at Kyoto University. She was a potter for some years before beginning to compose poetry. Her poetry books include *Empty Spring Houses* (1982), *The First Sunday in April* (1986), and *Milky Way* (1988).

Kiyoko Ogawa (née Sugiura) was born in Kyoto in 1952. She received her B.A. in English from Osaka University of Foreign Studies, her M.A. from Nara Women's University, and her Ph.D. from Hiroshima University. During 1982–83 she studied English literature at the University of Wuppertal in Germany. She started writing poems exclusively in English in 1982 and has self-published four books of poems—*The Poems of Kiyoko Ogawa* (1986), *Second Violin* (1990), and *Weed Paradise* (1992). She has been a member of the Poetry Society of Japan since 1986. In the academic field, she has written six essays on T. S. Eliot. She teaches English at Ritsumeikan University, Kyoto Sangyō University, and elsewhere. Mother of a daughter and married to a philosopher, she now resides in Ōtsu, near Kyoto.

Kyong Mi Park was born in Tokyo in 1956. She is a second-generation Korean and is now studying traditional Korean music and dance. Her first book of poems, *SOUP*, was published to critical acclaim in

1980. Her poems have appeared in various literary magazines, including *La Mer* and *Waseda Bungaku*. She is the Japanese translator of Gertrude Stein.

Yufuko Shima was born on the island of Amami Oshima in 1941. Her two books of poetry are *Wind Orchid* and *A Bridge to the Transparent Post*.

Ryōko Shindō grew up in Manchuria from the ages of one to nine. She coordinates a series of poetry readings and lectures that promote "a peaceful sense of the poetic" to counteract the effects of media bombardment on the senses. Her books of poems include *Rose Song* (1961), *Rose in the Light* (1974), and *Rose Letter* (1986).

Kazue Shinkawa was born in rural Ibaraki Prefecture in 1929. She studied poetry under the poet Yaso Saijō, who introduced many modernist poets, such as Amy Lowell and H.D., to Japan. Among her many published volumes, *Festival in the Field* won the Shōgakkan Literary Award in 1960, *Autumn in Rome* won the Muroo Saisei Poetry Prize in 1965, and *Ground Barley* won the Modern Poets Award in 1987. Shinkawa, former president of the Japan Modern Poets' Society, was coeditor of *La Mer*, an influential women's literary magazine.

Kazuko Shiraishi, born in Vancouver in 1931, received her education at Waseda University and the Iowa Writers' Workshop. She studied under Katsue Kitazono as a member of the VOU group, whose modernist experiments led her to adopt an American jazz-beat style in her works and readings. Her first book of poems, *Falling Egg City*, was published in 1951. With Kenneth Rexroth, she began the jazz/poetry revolution in Japan in the 1960s, giving collaborative readings and performances with jazz musicians such as John Handy, Sam Rivers, David McKay, and Frank Morgan and with poets such as Allen Ginsberg. Her works have been translated into English and many other languages, and she has given numerous readings and performances with jazz musicians around the world. She has participated in countless poetry festivals and conferences outside of Japan, including the Adelaide Festival of the Arts in Australia, the Afro-Asian Writers Symposium in Manila, the Rotterdam International

Poetry Festival in the Netherlands, the Portland Poetry Festival in Oregon, the UNESCO International Poetry Festival in Paris, the International Poetry Festival in Mexico, the "War on War" Poetry Festival in Milan, the Bisby Poetry and Jazz Festival in Arizona, and the Velmiki Poetry Festival in Bhopal, India. *Avant-garde* in both her poetry and lifestyle, she has written numerous volumes of poetry and been anthologized in dozens of collections. Outside of Japan, Shiraishi is Japan's best-known woman poet.

Harumi Makino Smith was born in Hokkaido in 1963. She has worked as an illustrator in Australia, taught English and worked as a waitress in a jazz cafe in Sapporo, and been a bookseller in Tokyo. In 1993 she published her first book of poems, *Usagi no Mimi*, which she translated into English ("Rabbit Ears"). Her second collection, *Kairan Shi*, is forthcoming. She has been writing poetry and novellas since high school, and is an avid record collector who feels that "creative music makes my work more progressive and brings it to another dimension." She has read her poetry at the Jayne Cortez Workshop at the Tokyo American Center, Chino Prison in California, the Alligator Lounge in Santa Monica, and CalArts in Valencia, California. She recently married the American jazz trumpeter and composer Wadada Leo Smith and moved to Southern California, where music continues to inspire her writing.

Fumiko Tachibana taught English for fourteen years at secondary schools and universities in Japan before she came to the United States, after ending her marriage of fifteen years. Writing poetry in English makes her "free of speech," she says. Her first poetry book, *To the Continent and Back*, was published in 1989 as a special issue of *Printed Matter* by New Leaf Press (now Saru). Her poems have appeared in *Poetry Nippon, Printed Matter, Midwest Poetry Review, Canadian Review, Portfolio*, and other journals. She lives in San Diego with her husband and son.

Chimako Tada is considered Japan's foremost intellectual poet. She is the award-winning author of over ten volumes of poetry and seven volumes of essays, as well as translations from the French of Saint-John

Perse, Georges Charbonnier, Antonin Artaud, and many works of
Marguerite Yourcenar, including *Memoires d'Hadrien.*

Junko Takahashi was born in Chiba Prefecture in 1944 and educated at
Tokyo University. She runs her own publishing company and works
as an editor as well as a translator of French poetry into Japanese.
Her main works are *Fireworks* (1956), *A Mock Chronicle* (1971), and *A
Lotus-Easter* (1980). Other books of poetry include *Not Letting Flowers
By* (1986) and *The Happy Leaf* (1990).

Taeko Tomioka is a popular poet, translator, novelist, and feminist essay-
ist. She was born in Osaka in 1935 and received her education at
Osaka Women's University, where she majored in English literature.
Since childhood, she has been interested in Jōruri (singing that
accompanies Bunraku, or puppet theater) and its dramatic dialogue.
Return Call (1959), her first book of poetry , received the "H"
Award in Poetry. Her other works include *Charismatic Oak Tree*
(1959) and *Girl Friends* (1964). Although Tomioka stopped writing
verse over twenty years ago to concentrate on fiction, her poetry con-
tinues to influence and inform generations of young women.

Mieko Watanabe was born in Tokyo in 1943 and received her education
at Keio University and Musashino Art College. She lived in Geneva
and Paris from 1987 to 1989. She has published four books of
poetry, the most recent being *Throat* (1985) and *Fever Attack*. A book
of translations, *Woman Loving*, was published in 1990 and a book of
essays, *What is Feminism?*, was published the same year. Watanabe is
also an award-winning painter.

Michiko Yamamoto was born in Tokyo in 1936 and studied Japanese lit-
erature at Atami Gakuen Junior College. A popular poet and novel-
ist, her books of poems include *Inside the Jar* (1957), *Green Sheep and
One* (1960), and *Sunday Umbrella* (1976). She lived in Australia from
1969 to 1971, and it was there that she started writing fiction. Her
novella *Betty-san* won the Akutagawa Award in 1972. Though her
main interest is now fiction, her poetry still continues to influence
many young poets.

Hiroko Yoshida is a poet and painter. She has published three books of poetry, and her paintings have been widely exhibited. She is the owner of a cafe/gallery in Tokyo's *shitamachi* district, the old "downtown" district that is the home of generations of artisans and tradespeople. The cafe is well known for its poetry readings, Butoh dance performances, and art exhibitions.

Sachiko Yoshihara was born in Tokyo in 1932 and educated at Tokyo University. Her first book of poems, *Childhood: Successive Prayer* (1964), won the Muroo Saisei Award, and her second and third books of poems both won the Takami Jun Award. Her most recent books of poems include *Dream or . . .* , *Night Flight*, and *The Day I Saw a Blackbird*. A former actress, Yoshihara is also a scriptwriter and director of Butoh, modern Japanese dance. She is interested in making poetry "cubic" through experimental readings that combine music and song with the spoken word. With Kazue Shinkawa, she coedited the influential women's literary magazine *La Mer* from 1983 to 1993. She has written over ten volumes of poetry and ten volumes of essays in addition to her many translations and children's stories.

Tsuneko Yoshikawa was born in Saitama Prefecture in 1939 and received her education at Waseda University. She has published six volumes of poetry and several volumes of essays. Her main works are *Songs in Praise of Life* (1958), *Rose and the Sea* (1960), and *Algeria* (1980). She is an instructor of French at Nihon Bunka University.

bibliography

Following is a selected bibliography of works about Japanese poetry in English. The anthologies were consulted in the preparation of this volume. For a comprehensive list of related publications, see the Bibliography in *A Long Rainy Season: Haiku and Tanka*, Volume I of this series.

INDIVIDUAL POETS

Gibson, Keiko Matsui. *Stir up the Precipitable World!* Translated by the author. Bilingual Japanese and English. Milwaukee: Morgan Press, 1983.

Ibaragi, Noriko. *When I Was at My Most Beautiful and Other Poems 1953–82.* Translated by Peter Robinson and Fumiko Horikawa. Cambridge, Mass.: Skate Press, 1992.

Kageyama, Yuri. *Peeling.* English-language original. Oakland: I. Reed Books, 1988.

Ogawa, Kiyoko. *Second Violin.* English-language original. Hiroshima: 1990.

——. *Weed Paradise.* English-language original. Ōtsu, Japan: 1992.

Shiraishi, Kazuko. *Burning Meditation.* Translated by John Solt. Tokyo: Seichōsha, 1986.

——. *Seasons of Sacred Lust.* Edited by Kenneth Rexroth and translated by Ikuko Atsumi, John Solt, Carol Tinker, Yasuyo Morita, and Kenneth Rexroth. New York: New Directions, 1978.

Smith, Harumi Makino. *Rabbit Ears.* Translated by the author. Green Valley, Calif.: Kiom Press, 1995.

Tachibana, Fumiko. *To The Continent and Back.* English-language original. Tokyo: Printed Matter Press, 1988.

Tada, Chimako. *Moonstone Woman: Selected Poems and Prose.* Translated by Robert Brady, Kazuko Odagawa, and Kerstin Videaus. Santa Fe: Katydid Books, 1990.

Tomioka, Taeko. *See You Soon: Poems of Tomioka Taeko.* Translated by Hiroaki Sato. Chicago: Chicago Review Press, 1979.

ANTHOLOGIES OF MODERN AND CONTEMPORARY JAPANESE LITERATURE AND POETRY

Atsumi, Ikuko, and Graeme Wilson, trans. *Three Contemporary Japanese Poets* [Shuntaro Tanikawa, Hitoshi Anzai, Kazuko Shiraishi]. London: London Magazine Editions, 1972.

Brower, Robert H., and Earl Miner. *Japanese Court Poetry.* Stanford, Calif.: Stanford University Press, 1961.

Davis, Albert R., ed. *Modern Japanese Poetry.* Translated by James Kirkup. Queensland: University of Queensland Press, 1978.

Fitzsimmons, T., and Yoshimasu Gozo. *The New Poetry of Japan.* Santa Fe: Katydid Books, 1993.

Hibbett, Howard. *Contemporary Japanese Literature.* New York: Alfred E. Knopf, 1977.

Keene, Donald. *Modern Japanese Literature: An Anthology.* New York: Grove Press, 1956.

————. *Dawn to the West: Japanese Literature in the Modern Era.* New York: Holt, Rinehart, and Winston, 1984.

Kijima, Hajime. *The Poetry of Postwar Japan.* Iowa City: University of Iowa Press, 1975.

Miller, Brian, and Taeko Kudo, trans. *Three Poets: Emori Kunitomo, Konagaya Kiyomi, Yoshihara Sachiko.* Tokyo: BT Books, 1987.

Morton, Leith. *An Anthology of Contemporary Japanese Poetry.* New York and London: Garland Publishing, 1993.

Ninomiya, T., and D. J. Enright. *The Poetry of Living Japan.* London: John Murray, 1957.

Ōoka, Makoto. *A Play of Mirrors: Eight Major Poets of Modern Japan.* Santa Fe: Katydid Books, 1987.

Rexroth, Kenneth, and Ikuko Atsumi. *The Burning Heart: Women Poets of Japan.* New York: Seabury Press, 1977. Reissued as *Women Poets of Japan.* New York: New Directions, 1982.

Sato, Hiroaki. *Ten Japanese Poets.* Hanover, N.H.: Granite Publications, 1973.

———— and Burton Watson. *From the Country of Eight Islands: An Anthology of Japanese Poetry.* New York: Columbia University Press, 1986.

Shiffert, Edith, and Yuki Sawa. *Anthology of Modern Japanese Poetry.* Tokyo: Charles E. Tuttle, 1972.

Ueda, Makoto. *Modern Japanese Poets and the Nature of Literature.* Stanford: Stanford University Press, 1983.